Yes, God. Vol. 1

Co-authored by:

Pamela Benson Owens

Alba Hatcher

Debby Krueger

Holly Fenney

Valena Spradley

Kathy Daniel

Barbara Hollace

Pearl Chiarenza

Liz Brewer

Renee Otiende

RichEtta Weathersbee

Colette Huxtable

[handwritten note: ...sed by the words of this book Debby Krueger 4/17/19]

Yes, God Vol 1

ISBN: 9781091802469

Saying YES is a choice.
It is a decision.
It is a daily walk.
What are you choosing to
say YES GOD to today?

Table of Contents

Saying Yes to God is truly a faith walk and often it can feel alone, scary, exciting and just a mix of things. But as you read each story, my prayer is that you are challenged, encouraged, inspired, comforted and confident that you will find strength in your journey. Let's choose to walk with a hope and a sense of faith that what you are believing God for He will hear and answer you.

Here's to Your Yes!

Kimberly Pitts
Founder, UImpact
www.uimpact.net

Pamela Benson Owens
Yes, God!

Share a yes God moment you have encountered where you had to trust Him without knowing all the steps.

My entire adult life for a while felt like cruel and unusual punishment moments where I had to trust God. The kind where one must consider just driving away from it all. The kind where you didn't want to adult and figure it out, the kind where it would have been easier to give up. I can recall ten of those moments that come to mind.

I've had many life plot twists that it would take years to share all of those moments. However, I look back on the period when I started my business. I selected this moment because it was hard but also because I continue to work through some that were even more difficult. One thing I've learned upfront about faith, it can't be rushed or short ordered and you can't skip steps. It doesn't work that way.

Let's be clear, I was nudged by God early on, I knew I would be an entrepreneur. Several instances in my childhood affirmed that. But, the entire process of starting a business was a gut-wrenching lesson in trusting God.

I went from a corporate job with a nice salary to a hard stop exit and a journal full of dreams. That's right folks, I had NO plan. Here is what I knew at that point: Saying yes to God was firmly planted in what you also must say no to. I was being undervalued, disrespected and underpaid compared to my counterparts who had less education. I was being passed up for job opportunities that were being parsed out to older white men with perhaps more experience, but who lacked energy and innovation and most times, basic leadership skills.

When you are in a situation like that, your faith is not only tested, the behaviors of the world can have you thinking something is wrong with you. It is the worst kind of mental abuse you can do to yourself. This is a big insult to God! To believe we are less than, unworthy, not smart enough, not pretty enough, not skinny enough, etc. It isn't true. God says we are worthy and built for greatness- done and dusted.

We deviate from this truth when we put ourselves in situations that are not for us (and I mean any situation including marriage), yet we try to force them to be. The rationale for doing this is because of the fear of the unknown and façade addiction. We don't want those around us to know the truth about our lives If we are operating in mind manipulations rather than faith functionality- we can wake up and find ourselves off in the ditch of life.

I've spent plenty of time there in the past and I'm intentional about not going back there. So, there I was, newly married and launching a business. It would be a consulting firm that focused on training and development through the lens of Human Resources support. Three days into my new life I thought: Oh my gosh, what have I done?

I've never become so focused in my life. Why? Because at the time it felt like, I only had two things going for me: My brain and God. When you need to figure out how you will contribute to the household to make ends meet, and oh actually have money to buy meat............ you get focused fast, real fast.

This is where my faith was tested and tried. This is when I spent a lot of time on my knees asking God to, "make it plain". I used to get up early in the morning and pray on the couch for a long time. In my mind, I had no room for teachable moments or error, so I asked God to guide my every step.

It worked! I was a millionaire in three months, and I made the Forbes 100 list in the first year. NOT.

What I got was a bunch of teachable moments lessons about how to run a business and more about developing my relationship with God and trusting Him.

Note: While we should not force things, God never promised us the road to success and well-being would be easy. As a matter of fact, the road to our destiny often feels like pushing rope uphill.

The hard knocks of starting and sustaining a business were tough. I wouldn't trade those moments for anything because those moments got me to where I am today. A rock-solid faith and a relationship with God that is put forth first in everything I do and say. Those are the moments that built me to be a more forgiving, compassionate, and an unrelenting follower of Christ. And, unapologetically so.

It doesn't mean I don't have white-knuckle moments trying to get it all done, or frustration with clients or exhaustion around completing proposals for new business. It means I wake up in pure gratitude for the journey and I go to bed at night praising God for what he brought me through. I also praise God for what he didn't give me, or when I didn't get my way, why? I've learned it wasn't mine for the taking.

The "yes" moments with God feel less and less about "blind faith" when you look back on God's track record. While how God answers prayers doesn't always resemble what I asked for, it is still an answered prayer. God respects your color coded, well thought out, life strategic plan but please know, he isn't going to follow what you want, when you want it and how you want it.

Looking back on a variety of life pivots, I was not ready for what I was asking God for. Talk about a merciful and marvelous God who would not give me what I thought I wanted but instead opted for giving me what I needed. I have even been able to rebound and grow from what felt like disappointment to praising God for saving me from myself- literally. If you stop and think about it, we all have "yes" God moments if we would only recognize them. If you are reading this and thinking all of your "yes" moments were orchestrated by you and you alone, you are arrogant. Not one person on this earth is masterfully navigating life on earth without a higher power. Let me rephrase that. Nobody who is navigating life with a mentality of abundance and joy is doing so at their own doing. Once we profess our love and belief in God, He partners with us for the long haul. If we would just remember that, our "yes" moments should be daily.

How did you develop your faith when it seemed like nothing was going right in your life? Share a situation where you had to develop your faith walk.

Over the course of my life I can name a variety of pockets of time where things were not going right in my life. But even now when I hear that statement "going right" it gives me pause. How do we define "going right"?

During a time when business was booming, and I had more clients than I could manage, it seems like things in my personal life went haywire. My father was diagnosed with Parkinson's at a young age and my dear Aunt Marilyn also young, was battling a cancer that had her body under full attack.

In between my travel schedule, which at the time was ridiculous, I was deeply worried about the two of them. There was a level of fear and concern- even guilt to a certain degree, every time I would leave to go make money. I had plenty of conversations with God- not always calm and pretty. I constantly asked God to share with me what was I to learn about why two people I loved so much, were suffering.

One day on the way back from a trip it occurred to me that the current situation with my aunt and my father were gifts and a stinging reminder of time. I walked away from a large client just days later, not because I didn't enjoy the work, but because I needed to spend time with my loved ones.

I look back on that now and think to myself, what took me so long to figure it out? I took a strategic sabbatical from my business to do the thing that God calls us to do: show love, compassion, mercy, and grace.

My busyness related to my work became a different kind of busy. Please note: when you stop working with clients, there is no money coming in. I figured God would work it out. I turned it over to God like a pancake in a skillet.

Guess what happened? Nothing. My business didn't fold. I didn't go bankrupt. My family had food and all the necessities and an occasional want.

Guess what I got? An opportunity to walk in faith during a very difficult time that ended in me becoming a faith warrior.

During my sabbatical I could take my father back and forth to his appointments in another city, sit bedside with him as he went through brain surgery, help care for him when he went through prostate cancer (yes shortly after his Parkinson's diagnosis), sit with him and get to know him in this new normal. The gift of conversation, sharing our concerns, laughing, and learning from each other on the commutes made me understand that even during the difficult time, God placed me where I needed to be. My concerns about money and resources faded because the time with my father was priceless.

While that was happening, I was burning up the highway back and forth to support my Aunt Marilyn. She was a fighter who just wanted to be treated normally. Her cancer had gotten deep into her bones and she spent a lot of days in pure pain. Whatever she asked for, I worked hard to make happen.

Four days after my 40th birthday, I sat bedside with her singing and praying with her. She was using a white board to communicate because she had such significant sores in her mouth from radiation it was painful to talk. I listened to her gasp and her chest raise from the bed for 7 ½ straight hours as she went into air hunger. I sang all of her favorite songs, we gathered around her and prayed multiple times, we read scriptures, we nodded as she wrote on the white board over and over, "I love you", I held her hand and looked her square in the eye affirming her salvation and her life well lived.

I held her hand until she drew her last breath. It was one of the hardest things I've ever done, yet the most life changing. Had I been more worried about my business and money, I would have missed these critical moments of sowing seed into important relationships in my life. The following week I secured new clients, and the work continued on…. without a hitch.

How did you stay motivated in a season where patience, faith and trust had to be exercised?

You won't find a more impatient person than me. I promise you. Even writing this chapter was difficult for me because I wanted to be done with it. I got all the way to the end of it and had to throw it in the trash. It wasn't what God wanted me to say, so I had to start over. Really God?

See, faith is just as much about being in relationship with God as it is about being obedient too. I know, I know we don't like that word, but it is a necessary word. I spent the earlier parts of my life being a "Yes, but…" gal. Yes God, but could you? Yes God, but I don't like her at all. Yes God, but can you just for once make carbs good for me? I realized that obedience can't be halfhearted or half way.

Submitting to God's will and way isn't weakness, it is surrendering to a higher and divine power that is way more qualified than I am to make things happen the way they need to. And let's face it, God has both a sense of humor and a real sobering way of getting His point across. Again, I'm stubborn and while I made significant progress, patience continued to be challenging for me. has never been one of my strong areas. In 2010, God fixed it and gave me the gift of a beautiful boy named Preston Alexander. My son was diagnosed with Autism and it threw me into the world of the unknown.

I remember waking up one morning and taking all volumes of the book, "What to Expect When You're Expecting" and throwing them in the trash. For those of you who are not familiar with these books, they outline the milestones that your child "should be" achieving by certain ages. For me it was a beacon of hopelessness and failure because Preston didn't walk, talk, or do anything else in the timeframe they suggested.

I had to replace my patience with God anointed persistence. My faith became the backdrop for every step I've taken and continuc to take with Preston. I had to trust the doctors and therapist to help navigate the way, but what I trusted the most, (because let's face it, humans are flawed), was God.

To this day, I am still defensive with my closest friends about Preston. Only one person ever asked me how I was doing during that time. I have now realized that when something of this magnitude happens, people are at a loss of what to do and say. Sure, people sent me books and cards and such, but nobody stopped to ask me how I was doing with all of this. Thankfully, my faith in God helped me put one foot in front of the other into territory I knew nothing about.

Spoiler alert: even when you activate your faith, patience and trust have to come along with it. It took Preston eighteen solid months of practicing before he ever could button his shirt. He started talking but is still in speech therapy, he now can be in a room with other people but still requires behavioral therapy. A steady rain outside can throw him off kilter for days because of the barometric pressure. Patience isn't optional.

I've had low moments where I've lost patience with him. There is nothing worse than those brown eyes looking up at you with a face that says, "I don't understand why you are acting this way Mommy." It is painful and through lots of prayers and patience, those moments have drastically reduced. I actively practice my faith daily because it is the gateway to peace.

What scriptures, books or resources do you recommend using when you are looking to grow in your walk with God?

I love when people ask me what books or resources I would recommend. I am an avid reader. At any given time, I'm reading several books. But, over the years I've changed my answer. The resource I recommend is the good ole' bible. It is full of wisdom and guidance, clarity and also opportunities to ponder. There are three scriptures I think are important to mediate over when strengthening your faith walk: Jeremiah 29:11, Psalm 139:14, Galatians 5:22-23. What? Are you upset I didn't provide the actual scriptures for you? Nope, not going to do it. The first lesson in strengthening your faith is opening the bible up for yourself, so with that- get to it!

Pamela Benson Owens

Pamela Benson Owens has served as President and CEO of Edge of Your Seat Consulting, Inc. for the last 20 years. In this capacity, Pam has toured around the US delivering customized training, strategic planning, fundraising consulting, human resources, keynote speaking and executive coaching for corporate clients, school districts, non-profits, higher education institutions, religious entities, and small businesses.

In January of 2018, Pam fulfilled a long-time dream of joining forces with esteemed colleague Fayruz Benyousef and now has a dual role of serving as the Vice President of Business Development for Fayruz Benyousef Consulting and Acting President/CEO of EOYS where she continues to oversee the overall direction and vision of the organization.

Known for her no-nonsense communication style, Pam holds an undergraduate degree from Texas A&M University and a Master's degree from St. Edward's University. She leverages the methodology from both degrees to create "teachable moments".

She calls Austin home and is married with two kids.

Alba Hatcher
Yes, God!

Each of us has a journey that God has taken us on, There are moments that occur along that journey that helped shape and define who we are. Share one of those. YES, GOD moments you had encountered where you had to trust HIM without knowing all the steps.

The Expectation of Gods Miracle.

How do you know when you've truly experienced a God moment vs coincidence? In the bible we hear about the miracles Jesus performed in his short time on earth; he turned water into wine, walked on water, healed a leper, cured a paralytic, opened the eyes of a blind man, and fed thousands from the portions of a small family meal. We carry an expectation for a God moment to be life altering and grand in gesture, like a military man who finds honor in putting to rest his lifelong furry friend; a man you would otherwise never see cry, is in tears when he couldn't find the shell round that took his friends' life; in that moment a bird briefly lands on his shoulder, fly's, and lands on the ground just a few feet in front of him and fly's away; astonished to find the bird had landed on the shell round he was grieving over and looking for. This is a true story but even the grand moments don't always change a man (or woman). Messages from God don't always come this obvious. Sometimes we must look for them. We must be in tune for them and we must be *willing* to hear His message.

People experience little miracles every day. Unfortunately, they often go unnoticed; the moment of delay at a street light because you've dropped your phone, at that moment another vehicle runs the red light, saving you from death; the anonymous gift from church when you weren't sure if you'd make bills, finds you with enough for the entire family Christmas and weeks' worth of groceries; the woman who decides life for her unborn child... It can almost seem like these moments only ever happen to someone else. We see versions of miracles on YouTube but like watching from afar; we forget how close those moments truly are to us. When we lose faith or are in a season of grief, unforgiveness or any other emotional property that makes you human, we can sometimes get lost. However, no matter what, and by Gods amazing grace, we can always come back to Him.

My YES GOD story was not an easy one to share. It's one that for many years I kept private, ashamed by my own weaknesses but one that I felt could not be truer to the reality of being human. All humans make mistakes. All humans feel pain, shame and struggle in their life. I pray that this story can be an encouragement to women struggling to find the balance in their marriage. To the woman that feels like she lost herself somewhere along the way, needing to be confident in who she is, as a mother, wife and career driven, but foremost a child of God, Chosen. The choice of prayers, actions and communication will be what shape the opportunity of a great marriage, the triangle that as you and your spouse grow closer together, you also grow closer to God.

My husband and I were still new in marriage when I found my calling. I had spent years being lost and uncertain of who I was. We struggled with learning how to love each other, how to be compatible in our new home, meld families, meld traditions, meld two very different ways of approaching life. When I lost my way, it was him that encouraged me to pursue a hobby, something I loved to do. "Why don't you try to do what you used to love?" He said. At the moment I was surprised, somehow thinking that was not part of the plan, naïve in not fulling understanding the definition of a marriage.

I was 18 when we got married. I had never been in a boyfriend/girlfriend relationship for over 2 weeks. In high school, I would date a guy for a week, in that week, know I didn't want to be with him anymore, and then give him the second week to try to make it up. When he didn't (they never did), I dumped him. With my husband it was different. I remember receiving a text from him that said, "Happy 3 Month Anniversary!" I was shocked. Had it been that long? Wait a minute, did I see something that made we want to break up with him... Nope! Mutual friends, hobbies and outings; sometimes we would sit under the stars together for hours, one day he said I should be up there. 'My beautiful girl' so it could last forever, just like the stars. We had, as I saw, the sweetest dating relationship.

One day I was riding in the car, coming back from a movie with my dad, when I said, "I think he's the one". My dad being used to my previous way of dating said, "no wait, you need to break up with him" and for weeks he tried to tell me it was time to break up, he wasn't good enough according to my dad, yet I said no. It came down to an ultimatum, 'Break Up or Move Out'. I happily chose the latter. Harry and I moved in together, however with his family coming from a conservative Christian family, they said we couldn't live together without being married. We soon after started pre-marital counseling and on our last day the pastor said all that was left to do was chose a date, we said "How about Friday?" It was the most beautiful and romantic young love story, the kind that could make a book into a movie, I even bought him that star we talked about while dating as a gift. But most movies stop at the happy ending, they don't share the part that comes next.

We fought a lot. Mostly at my stubbornness of not being accepting of his love, not feeling like I was enough, while my family and I today have a wonderful relationship and I wouldn't trade any minute of our history, it wasn't always on the happy story side. I struggled with finding my happiness. I lost touch with friends. For a while, our unapproved marriage lost me all contact with my family. I felt alone, trapped and without a sense of purpose. As I mentioned before it was my husband that encouraged me to get back into the things I loved most when we first met. I tried martial arts and realized that I had grown out of it and went back to dance. I reached out to a woman that I knew owned an all-women's gym, I used to dance with her, teach her choreographies, when I asked her if I could teach a women's dance class and create it to fit into a fitness setting, she loved it! Within no time I was there full time, every day I had women asking me how I should workout this, what should I be eating, all the while I was still 65lbs overweight, what on earth were these ladies doing asking me. In the moment I was happy and content with teaching dance, and I would figure the rest out later.

To my husband, there I was, enjoying something, working late because I wanted to, in a whirlwind of change neither of us were ready for. So, when the time came, believe it or not, poor communication made my husband who was supposed to be the first, instead, the last to know.

The day I decided to become a trainer, I walked into my boss's office and started with "hey, so I've been thinking…". She spent the next hour pulling words out of me. Question after question, almost testing me, was this the right path for me? It was an insightful and necessary conversation to recognize my goals and direction in this new venture I planned on pursuing. I walked out of that office feeling empowered. I was going to drop this excess weight that stress of not 'being me' had put on. Plus the weight of living and working by someone else's standards. I would help other women do it too and feel as free as I did in that moment. I spent the day researching; what did I need to do? How much money would I need? What would be my plan once I become certified? I even started my consulting paperwork! I wrote the questions I wanted to ask the ladies that came to see me. I made notes on what I wanted to learn about them, and how was I going to find the trigger that made them lose who they were. I was sitting in the business parking lot in my run-down SUV when I told him I had it all figured out. My life and everything leading to this moment had finally made sense, but I forgot to make my husband a part of it. Perhaps he was scared. Scared because this isn't where he thought I would be led, scared because he didn't know or care for the boss that introduced me into a new lifestyle and some of my biggest life decisions. Scared because he didn't know or understand what this meant to me. And scared because, as his wife, I shared none of it. I let my previous hurts overflow into my marriage. Hurts that taught me sharing was the enemy. So, when he said that is not a real career, you can't do that, or make money in that. I heard someone else's voice. Truly the voice of several in my life that said I couldn't do something. I self-destructed. And in that line of defense, as a young woman what I had done at every moment prior that hurt me, I left him.

During these months of separation, the boss that once motivated me turned sour. What I thought was God's will, wasn't. That was made clear; the enemies promise will never deliver. God's promise does! Within a few short months that boss of mine closed the doors to her business, as I said goodbye to the location of my start in the industry. What's worse is she left behind hundreds of customers without a notice or care, only a sign on the door. Looking back, I should have known! No fret though, she had a plan. She had a vision of a new business, bigger, better, luxury style just the way she really would have loved it to be from the beginning. I continued to work for her, but the process was a headache. Her brain was scattered with specs of success but never a full picture. Her life was a mess, but she made it look glorious. As a young 21-year-old, I accompanied her to parties, surrounded by luxury, shopping experiences as if from a movie and all the while she said we were 'networking' although rarely did business ever come up. I was being paid to have fun, who wouldn't want that life. For a time, I looked up to her, I valued her opinion, but it was the gift wrap of success, money and fame, never the real deal, appearance on the outside. In the process of day to day work, meals and chore tasks she had me on, our conversations would lead to personal things, my sharing areas of unhappiness, she always reminded me of negativity, all the while pushing me away from my husband. The devil had a hold on me and used her as a venue of destruction. She showed up the day I moved out, asked me to move in with her, something in my mind told me not to. I knew her level of dishonesty, often speaking ill of the people she claimed to care about. I saw how she ended friendships, business relationships, always ugly and hateful. Again, I should have known. In a time when I was hurt, I turned to what looked like could lead to happiness. I left behind memories, I left behind promises, promises to God, I left behind the dream I built with my husband. Some of which I would never get back the same way and some of which would begin in a whole new way.

During this time of transition, I was living with my parents. They attempted to talk to me, but it seemed to fall on death ears. Over and over I would justify my choice because he didn't come after me. I literally fell behind blinders, a tunnel vision of negativity with no light shining down any tunnels. My light was gone but that's because God was not where I was looking to. Even though marriage is a two-way street, I saw only one. All I wanted was for him to break down the door, hold me and never let go, never let go no matter how much I pushed him away. That was the picture in my head, fairy tale land I wished to come true. My birthday passed which he didn't acknowledge. Didn't I deserve it? I was furious but I knew my answer. The following month I saw he ran a mud run, a mud run without me which I wanted and had asked him to do with me. I saw moments, moments that were supposed to be MY moments. That same week, it was the week of his birthday, he delivered something to the house. I opened the card and just cried, not the way you would think. I cried out of anger and yelled. My mother walked in inquiring for obvious reasons. I wanted so bad to tear up that card, something told me not to, probably my mother. She read the card and tried to reason with me, I saw nothing but negativity, hurt and depression, so far deep nothing else made sense or even occurred to me.

Back at my boss's house I was having internal battles with myself. In business she wanted high luxury, high security, were talking showers that were also tanning beds. She also encouraged me to date other men, shared stories about her own experiences with men. In that moment it stopped feeling right. I looked at her life, as glamorous as it was, it wasn't me. Her stories were not what and how I wanted to live. Her lifestyle not my lifestyle. Her men, not my man. By this point I had already reached my health and fitness goals of losing the 65 pounds. I was eating clean-ish, exercising regularly, and from what anybody could tell on the outside I looked healthy. I was proud of that about myself, Afterall, I worked hard for it. I didn't have hundreds of dollars to spend on a single training session, multiple sessions a week, like the plans she built within her own business model. Friendships had no true meaning to her, at least not by what I would define friend in a friendship. No. Money would not be successful in the ability to buy happiness no matter how hard she tried. The same woman that had once inspired me; she wanted to help women have a safe way to lose weight after a botch surgery left her wheelchair bound for 2 years, well she had just scheduled another, more invasive, unnecessary, cosmetic surgery. That was my switch. All this work to go towards making a difference in people's lives, mind body and soul while she was out doing it in all the wrong ways, a giant lie. What was I doing there? Why was I listening to her? Why didn't I leave sooner?

Don't ask me why I didn't leave sooner, why all those other incidents weren't a red light. I don't know, I look back and try to figure out what kind of mask was put over my head. My decision and two weeks' notice turned ugly fast. Complete with cease and desist letters, all of which held no merit but stressful nonetheless, harassment claims, cops called, so much drama, so many low blows. For example, I had started a continuing education course, her and I enrolled in the same course together. One week, I receive a call that I could not return to class. I knew what it came down to. She had money. She could spend lots of money with this institution, she had financial backing complete with attorneys willing to let her waste their time and she put up enough a fuss; they didn't want any trouble. The business caught in the middle had a decision to make. Not to worry, it all worked out. At the time, I was hurt but something else amazing happened. The director of that course agreed to meet with me one on one. I completed the course and moved forward, she didn't.

One day back home, my life at this point is filled with drama, lies, grief, stress to the nines and the list goes on. I was hurting, feeling so alone in life I asked my soon-to-be not-husband if I could come see Harley. Harley was my dog, a German Shepard I begged for from the first moment he jumped placing both paws right on my stomach as if we were dancing. The day I went to see Harley, Harry, my still-husband was there, he ignored my presence while I shared my moment with the dog. It was then that I heard a voice. I looked to the dog, no he's not talking to me. "I'm right here." it said. I looked up at my still-husband, no, he said nothing, he has headphones on looking opposite of me. Again, "I'm right here." I cried as the voice continued. Images of the last 4 months and each time with the voice "I'm right here." He was there when I made the call to pursue a passion of dance. He was there when I had my interview to work at the gym full time. He was there when I decided to turn my whole life around to a healthier lifestyle and become an influence to others. He was there when I didn't engage in negatively speaking about others. He was there while I was being attacked. He was the voice that reminded me to stay true to myself. He was there when the drama occurred. He protected me from the hurt of the world's words. He was there to make sure I still had an education. He was there to see me finish my coursework. He was there knowing it would become my lifelong career choice of helping others. He knew what I didn't, that I would learn how to accredit it all back to Him in the human design that He made from the beginning. He was there as a voice of kindness, a voice that understood my pain and knew my heart. As I sat there with our dog Harley, I prayed, a prayer that sounded much like, 'I messed it all up, what should I do?' God answered with my physical inability to move and before I knew it words came out of my mouth. Words that would be heard by the man I had years prior promised to share my life with, words to the man that I had hurt months prior. Now I can't tell you what those words were, but I do remember that night I got my answers, the why, the how, and I small glimpse of what next. That night started the process of dropping everyone in my life that didn't serve the good in life. Steered back in direction of where God wanted me to be and let Him take the wheel.

Reframing business for me was easy. First of all, it was only me that had to decide. I let passion drive me. Everything that I wanted the business to be I made it happen on my terms. I let God in, and He made it flourish. Even when I wasn't sure, even when to others it didn't make sense, it made sense to me and I went for it. Along the way I had my reminders to trust God, and He has. God has always provided, someway somehow, even when I lost business clients, He always made sure there was money in the bank account. His voice leads me to my business slogan, which lead my business direction, which made the difference for making a difference. None of that would have been possible without Him.

Reframing marriage on the other hand, not easy. Building up two hurt people to become one non-hurt couple. The first two years were an uphill battle. Layers of rebuilding trust, communication of pain to get past hurt, opening my heart and allowing myself to be vulnerable, knowing anything could happen. My fear of self-hurt had to be replaced with a mutual understanding. I could do all this and just might open myself to the opportunity to be destroyed well beyond anything I had experienced or dished out, but a risk worth taking. Tunnel vision of negativity was replaced with growing anew in Christ, faith to walk with my eyes closed, not knowing what would come next, discovering light, the good, and always seeking it, Him, first. God made communication possible, patience possible, understanding each other possible. God gave me a man that would support my life altering decision that to me is not only a business but continues giving. I had to put in the work first of honoring Him and then honoring my husband. The note, my husband gave me during our time apart, the one I was angry over. Now being free from the blinders the enemy placed upon me; that note goes with me everywhere I go, it stays in my wallet always, it reads "I love you Alba, I will be here waiting to fight for you and be the man you want me to be once you're ready and open your arms and heart to me. I will always be with you within the stars, we are in the same constellation together, Always & Longer than Forever. Love Now & Always, Harry. Attached to that, a certificate from the International Star Registry.

Oh, and years later I found out, my dad, the man who thought Harry could never be good enough for his little girl, went to him and planted the seed in my husband's mind to bring us back together. Yes. God. Was. There.

How did you develop your faith when it seemed like nothing was going right in your life? Share a situation where you had to develop your faith walk.

God has saved my life more times than I'm willing to admit. I've had many moments of complete breakdown, times that I didn't even want to live, and Jesus always came through and comforted me. God comes through in little ways, a friend sends you a message, you get a phone call and the person on the other line says "I felt like I needed to call you" what a blessing it is when the people in your life are in tune with God even when you are not. The only things that make life better are always in God's presence. 'The faith of a mustard seed can move mountains' right, when nothing is going right in my life, I will purposefully try reaching to God outside of my comfort zone, because that's where I have the opportunity to grow. I wanted to serve in the church, but I wasn't sure how, I went to a woman's conference with battles of self-hatred and lack of forgiveness. There a woman prayed over me like I have never experienced in my life. Just minutes prior, as the speaker spoke, I wrote some notes down as she invited ladies to the alter, I wrote key words; Beautiful, worthy, enough, the list went on with another 10 words along the same lines. As I walked to the alter, without saying a word, I handed her the paper. She quickly read it and asked, "what is this", I said "I need to believe these things". She prays for me but then stops and says, I feel like there is someone more, is there someone you need to forgive, and for the first time I said the names out loud, Erica, Will, Greer, dad, mom, Abe, Erin, Nick, Mark, Chris, myself, the list kept going, the list of every person who made me feel like I was nothing, who hurt me, they had no power over me anymore. At that moment, as if on purpose and reserved just for me, my favorite song came on, 'What a Beautiful Name'. This mattered because it's the song that always warms my soul, it was a comfort and reminder that He was with me when all this occurred and that He ultimately protected me through it all. This moment was the only time that song was played all weekend.

That experience. I want to help people experience something like that. I went home and became a member of the prayer team. Completely outside of my comfort zone! Negative thoughts tried to come at me but held no bearing. What a beautiful name for which nothing can stand against, the name of Jesus.

Forgiveness is what I've found can change EVERYTHING. Forgiving yourself when things didn't quite go the way you have liked or expected; what a silly burden to bear when life so clearly will move on. Remember God will still be God no matter what happens. Forgiving those who hurt you; what a relief it is. Holding fear because of something someone else does, only allows them to continue to have a hold on you. Why give them that power? Allow no one the ability to rob you from your future. Holding back because of fear falls under the same note. "I'm no longer a slave to fear, I am a child of God"

How did you stay motivated in season where patience, faith and trust had to be exercised?

EVERYTHING happens for a reason and a season; this includes the good, the bad, and everything in between. When events happen, even the events that are filled with pain, it's part of His plan. It may be something you need to learn, discovering new levels of strength or a process of life that we may not understand in the moment but often is revealed to us when He feels were ready to receive the information.

In my marriage it was the strength I had to find from within to stick out the hard times. Keeping it simple, I had to ask myself, what do I want? With that answer then, Ok, make it happen! Having a, or many, conversations with God, finding where you're supposed to be, and saying 'OK God, now use me for your greater good'. When I'm tired of trying, God gives me rest. When nothing makes sense, God gives me peace. When all I want to do is quit, God says otherwise.

I wear a bracelet that says, "God is Stronger" whatever the struggle, whatever the worry, God has it and is greater and stronger than anyone, anything, any circumstance that might come my way. I have forgiven; therefore, I am free.

What scriptures, books, or resources do you recommend using when you are looking to grow in your walk with God?

I tend to be busy but that's no excuse because when does God ever say, 'no sorry, I'm too busy for you right now'. Periodically I will participate in a women's group or bible study that keeps me focused and on schedule with weekly reading and meetings that keep me accountable. Our bible studies usually include questions within a book that reference the Bible or just straight up Bible. With that the ladies of the group discuss, enlighten, fellowship and trigger different thoughts or outlooks. It's amazing what you learn about yourself from listening to other people. Insights or different ways of thinking and opinions within a space of trust.

"Shine bright like the stars in the universe as you live out the word of life" Philippians 2:15b-16 this is a scripture I live by, if at any point I feel as though I am not fulfilling this then I'm on the wrong course.

Woman to Woman - Mom to Mom I recommend;

Unglued by Lysa Terkeurst. For your sanity. *The 5 Love Languages of Children.* Whether you've read the spouse, teenager, or other versions available, each book holds a unique perspective. Do not make the mistake of disregarding one because you've read another. You'll get something out of each, I promise! Read 1 Corinthians 13:4 in a new way. Instead of "Love is Patient, Love is Kind…" Replace it with "I AM Patient, I AM Kind…" and so on. I know for myself completing the first line can be quite the task! A beautiful and easy to remember reminder!

As a Wife I recommend:

The 5 Love Languages by Gary Chapman. This book is a complete game changer and saved my marriage, friendships, ties with the family. It also has a 'for children', 'for teens' versions. Over time, I have owned at least 5-7 copies of this book. I'll gift one to a friend or family member and then I need to buy another copy which also gets passed along. It's one of those!

For Women Only | For Men Only by Shaunti Feldhahn. Excellent insight in how men think and for the husband, how women think. This book highlights on the differences between men and women and their thinking process for finances, intimacy, multitasking, and many more!

The Power of a Praying Wife by Stormie Omartian. This book is a simple nightly read of just a few pages. Each night discusses a new topic you may pray about for your husband, in your husband. It also highlighted the simple truth that I can not change the man I fell in love with, I only have control over myself, my reaction, my response, and my faith to hand it over to God. Learn to meet your husband at the foot of the cross.

Read Ephesians 5:21-33 The roles of a husband and a wife. We as women want love, men see love through respect. Philippians 4:8 *"Whatever is true, whatever is noble, whatever is right, whatever is pure, whatever is lovely, whatever is admirable – if anything is excellent or praiseworthy – think about such things."* In my notebook I wrote an example for each line. It was a way to help me remember the good, even on the days when husband or anyone else for that matter are driving you mad, you can call to mind the good.

Proverbs 31:10-31 The goals of every wife, in God's word.

God is Within Her, She will Not Fall.

Alba Hatcher

Alba's journey has embodied the pathway of her life purpose. Growing up in martial arts she obtained a 3rd degree black belt, taught for six years; was a professional belly dancer, choreographer, and performer with renowned artists from eastern countries. Following many commitments and found fame, for a few years she observed herself overweight, unhappy and un-empowered like many women experience in life. Alba started teaching dance at an all-women's gym obtaining a leadership position. Every day she had new and frequent visiting women asking questions regarding fitness and overall wellbeing. In efforts to have answers she took a personal training course at The Cooper Institute while beginning her own personal journey; losing 65 pounds, keeping it off, continuing to educate herself, while surrounded by the best the fitness industry has to offer. She became a biomechanics specialist finding her passion for rehabilitation and corrective exercise. After completing the prestigious Ortho-Kinetics® course she was provided with the skills to find imbalances, looking at the human body as a work of art, created by God in all its natural healing beauty. She took this belief as she became a Licensed Bodywork Therapist in Texas, and now uses a combination of manual therapy and corrective exercise to help alleviate pain associated with previous injuries, surgeries, and habitual causes. Alba has been able to help hundreds by believing each person was placed on this earth for a specific purpose. As a natural born teacher, she continues to share her skill sets with professional trainers and individuals with the mutual desire to make the world a better, happier, healing, and inspirited place. Alba is a devoted wife, mother of two, serves as an active role in her church, and volunteers for various community and nationwide organizations. She is blessed with every opportunity to be a part of someone's journey and help them achieve what they never thought possible.

Debby Krueger
Yes, God!

Today I find myself 12 years into my grief journey after losing my husband Garry. Believing myself to be an independent woman and able to handle anything, I was shocked and not prepared. Not that I could have been or imagined the changes in me or my life that would become a reality. In the beginning, I didn't know who I was: my confidence, joys, likes, passions and loves were gone. Early on I thought, with my heart broken and part of myself missing I would struggle to become whole, but I'd learn to live a new life. As a woman of God, it would be hard to lose Garry, but I would be ok. I am not only ok now but more. More what? More of everything. I'm more faithful, a better listener, more patient and more. Not until I experienced my darkest places and believed I was never to recover did I grow and become more. I would die unto myself over and over as I learned to trust the Lord even more. This journey gave me the opportunity to say Yes to God often. In fact, I don't know how I would have made it if I hadn't had God.

This chapter will focus on the fulfillment of a vision I first documented in my journal in August 2008, two years after Garry's death. I will include some of my walk-in grief and how God knitted my life together as he weaved the good and the ugly together to create a better me and life. Having God at my side did not stop my pain or prevent me from terrible darkness but as it says in 2 Corinthians 12:9, *"But he said to me, My grace is sufficient for you, for my power is made perfect in weakness."* John 16:22 says, *"Now is your time of grief, but I will see you again and you will rejoice, and no one will take away your joy.* "I had to **Breathe** new life into my soul . You will find out as you join me on this journey.

By 2008 a lot had gone on in the last 2 years, I had healed some, but the journey was still hard. The first year I tried to make it through the day and get things back to normal **and** keep things the same. That was impossible because Garry wasn't here, and he added so much to my life. He was my spice, and I was his spirit. The second year was harder than the first. I always thought it would get better soon in the first year and by then, I knew it would take longer, maybe never would I feel whole again. Loving and following Jesus, I thought I would get my joy back, but it hadn't come back. I had stopped going to church because I couldn't sing because I had no joy and that was heartbreaking in its own way. I was still talking to God even though many times it was more like yelling at him. Thank goodness God is greater than me and able to do all things even when I felt so lost. Feeling lost never meant I was alone. God continued to hold me even when I yelled at him or when I fell into despair. God was always there.

Everyone wanted me to snap out of it because they loved me. They hated to see me in such pain, but it wasn't that easy. I would love to have felt better, but I had a hole inside and I was so empty. I could work but I found joy in nothing. I would work and take care of business, but I had become a homebody and did not engage with people unless I had too. My mom and sister, Diane were worried. So, they invited me to a day at the spa. We spent the day together. They knew I loved massages and it was a beautiful place. It had to make me feel better, right? I enjoyed the time there, but it did nothing to bring joy or the change in me we all wanted. But that was the day that God put a thought in my head that would not go away. That "vision" would change me even though it would take years to be realized.

At the spa, I sat on the balcony that day, rocking and looking at the river, I realized how blessed I was. I knew mom and Diane wanted me to feel better. This day reminded me I was blessed to have people who loved me even in my pain. I realized that my pain was great, and this had been the worst thing I had lived through but at least I had God, my family and people who loved me. Even though I had this knowledge, it didn't make me feel loved or help me snap out of it. I felt so alone. The blessing was that during this time and for what I call "the lost years" (the years after Garry died when I didn't feel like me) I realized that God was with me even though I felt alone. Most days I could find good in a day. Some days I didn't feel thankful for much, but I thanked God for something. That day I thanked him for all I had in people and provision even though I didn't feel whole or myself, just wounded and alone.

The next day, I continued to think about the day, and I came up with a "vision" or maybe I should say God planted a seed in my soul. It remained there. At the time I didn't realize this was for me as much as others. Now I know it was as much for me as for others. This vision was to help others, but the way God works it helped me first. This vision has stayed with me and given me something to work and plan for even though it took a long time to happen. It gave me something to hope for. **Breathe Retreats** would become part of my healing and when completed, help for others who would suffer grief.

I planned my "Breathe Retreat". I had a vision statement, planned activities, wrote a poem and drew a map for what I needed to add to my yard to make it perfect. My house was already a place with peace and comfort. I was ready to go.

The Vision Statement on August 8, 2008

To offer those suffering an experience where they would physically and spiritually feel God by the love and service of others during their time of need.

Breathe
By Debby Krueger

Be still

Remember who loves you

Each day talk to God

Accept help

Thank God for your blessings

Heal thyself

Enjoy the rest of your life!!

Quote from my journal.

"I know this one day of peace and being served will not end your grief, solve all your problems but it is a physical and spiritual way for you to know and feel that God is with you and know he will never leave you. My hope was this day would be a memory they could pull up on their hardest day and know God was with them."

As the seed grew, I was excited and knew there was something special about this plan. It was personal. It was like a prescription for grief that God gave me. I realized this poem had power and meaning.

Breathe: The title was important because before Garry's death I had learned how to use deep breathing to bring about calmness as I practiced being a presenter for parents and teachers. Two weeks after D-day (Garry's death day) to get things back to normal, I went to a Christmas Staff party with friends. As we walked to the door, laughing was evident even through the closed door. I wanted to turn and run, my stomach was churning. I stayed and as I walked through the door, I kept on walking (it felt like running) in search of a safe escape. It turned out to be a dark room with an open door and uncluttered wall. There I pressed myself against the wall and did my deep breathing. As I regained my composure, I could join the others. Was it a joyous occasion? Not for me but it was a step to healing. Breathing became a tool, God gave me even before it would be a precious tool for survival. Now, he wanted me to share it with others. In any stressful situation I can practice deep breathing while I drive or sit in a busy room. Earlier I needed the dark and wall to protect me and help me through the episodes of loss of control, fear, or anger that would overcome me. Breathing was part of the vision. Breathing would help me stay in the present and live. God wanted me to continue to use this myself and share with others.

Be Still: This refers to the verse Psalm 46:10, *" Be still and know I am God"*. I have called this my verse for years. I know it is everyone's, but I claim it often. I have carried it in my purse for over 35 years and its always served me well. After being still and breathing, I could be in the present and could then remember that God was in control; he would handle it. I stood on his omnipotence and promises to give me direction instead of the crazy out of control thinking that was in my head at the moment.

Remember who loves you: God always loves us even when we don't love ourselves or feel loved. I also had lots of people who loved me even in my pain even though I didn't feel loved. Sometimes I pushed people away, but I knew they wanted me to feel better. I was never alone even though I felt like it. This was and is still important to my walk.

Each day talk to God: Walking closer to God makes the journey easier. I know it sounds crazy but sometimes I would talk to God and give up whatever was on my mind and the next day nothing changed but everything had. That is God's grace being sufficient. We can't understand it, but I can stand on His promises. The more I read meditations, the Bible, and talked to God and others who believed, the more I knew of God's promises and what he wanted from me as his child. The Bible is relevant today and it can make a difference when you read it.

Accept help: I had always been good at helping but accepting and asking for help, no way. The hardest lesson to learn was to ask and accept help. There are so many verses about helping your neighbor in the Bible. Most people know helping others is a good thing even if they don't believe in Christ. So why is it so hard for us to accept help? If we know that it's good to help, then it must be important to receive that help. Here's the problem, if I was helping and doing things, I thought I was in control. I don't like to be vulnerable, but we all are, regardless of how independent you are. God is in control and the evils of sin wreak havoc in our world. We are vulnerable but once you accept that God is all powerful you can trust him and recognize that his help comes in all different and crazy ways. God does make life interesting.

Thank God for your blessings: I have had a blessed life, but it hasn't always been easy. There had been my brother's health challenges when I was a child, depression and loss of death for both my husband and myself but life was good. Believe it or not, I thought I was pretty much in control and made things work out like that. Garry's death was the first time in my life that I had no answers or way to deal with the loss. My brain knew a lot, but my heart didn't know how to handle this loss. It made my world look bleak and definitely out of control and with my confidence gone I could do little. I couldn't think of what to be thankful for, but every day I did I was better. It's hard but I would find something good. Sundays were always a hard day and being alone was hardest on that day. At one point I finally could say I was thankful for being alone because I could watch whatever I wanted on TV. Life is good and bad, but when we can find something to be thankful for it keeps our heart lighter.

Heal thyself: The message here is I had to work to heal myself. No one else could do it for me. Yes, there is help but you or I must take the steps. Some steps are very painful, but we must move, or you can get stuck and it keeps you from being all God wants for you. You must decide what helps you and who to ask for help. Every time I encountered a problem or fear, I would come up with a plan in case it happened again. Sometimes just having the plan made things better. I had a panic attack while driving very early in my grief. It was caused by a song on the radio. It was like I had never listened to music on the radio. All the songs had meaning I never felt before. Songs had potential to send me off in thought or panic. My decision was that if that ever happened again, I would just pull over. But before that, I decided that it was too early to drive, and I stayed home a lot and to drive in Austin I would have to ask for help. It helped me. It kept me and others safer, and I wasn't alone as much. It gave me contact I did not reach out for most of the time. My brain didn't think like it used to so problem solving helped me get back to thinking clearer.

Enjoy the rest of your life!! Again, hope is the message. I stand on God's word,

John 12:46 *"I have come into the world as a light so no one who believes in me should stay in darkness"*.

Proverbs 3:5-6, *"Trust in the Lord with all your heart and lean not on your own understanding; in all your ways acknowledge him and he will make your paths straight"*.

Matthew 28-30, *"Come to Me, all who are weary and heavy-laden, and I will give you rest. Take My yoke upon you and learn from me, for I am gentle and humble in heart; and you shall find rest for your souls. My yoke is easy and my load light".*

Jeremiah 29:11, *"For I know the plans I have for you," declares the Lord, "plans to prosper you and not to harm you, plans to give you hope and a future."*

John 10:10b, *" I come that they might have life, and that they might have it more abundantly."*

I realized that God had not brought me this far and given me Garry to love and help me grow to leave me in despair. There had to be more, I was not on this earth to love only one person. Yes, I loved and still love Garry. God has a plan and staying in despair couldn't be the answer. I worked, prayed and followed the prescription of this poem and today I can say I have joy again. I stood on the Promises of God and I still do. I will continue to follow God and enjoy my life serving him.

I was protective of my vision because it was personal. I shared it with a few people mostly other widows in my life. The interior designer helping me had lost her husband. I told her I had a vision/plan but didn't share it for a while. My confidence had been crushed in the lost years, I didn't trust my ideas. She said, "That's ok, tell me when you are ready, and that God will affirm it if it is from Him. In the next few months I told about 6 women about my plan. The more I talked about it the more anxious I got. Then one day, I remember hearing this message "Take care of yourself, you are not ready. Heal yourself." I knew it was God, I don't know how but I knew everything still seemed hard and this was a big plan. It would have overwhelmed me. I think the poem was for me to help me heal myself so one day I could help others and I do now.

Life went on and I continued to grow and gain in confidence. Then in August 2009, I had another blow. My brother who I was guardian for died. I did not know if I could go through grief again. God knew this too. It would not be the paralyzing grief I experienced with Garry, but it had the potential to set me back. Days after my brother's death, I heard my dream job came open; I had wanted and even written a job description and presentation to administration years before for the job. I applied for the job. I always wanted to work with parents and teachers helping them to improve their working relationships. I was hesitant about applying but decided I had to try. I was getting stronger. I needed to get out on my own and see if I could think and create again. Getting this job was a good transition for me and it helped me grow my income for retirement.

I enjoyed the new opportunity. My experience and desire to be in this position was intact but my passion was not like it had been. I continued to work this job for 4 years. My health declined, and I was having panic attacks at work. I was working so hard and felt like I was hitting my head against a brick wall. I made progress in my job, but my passion and health were failing. I ended up in the hospital and on FMLA for most of the spring.

During this time, I never forgot my vision and I was taking a more active part in a nonprofit called The Christi Center. It was the grief center where I received help after

Garry's D-day. Now, I would take others on their first visit. I was interested in joining the development board for the Christi Center. In fact, the day they officially asked me to be on the development board was the day I found out that I did not have a job for the next year. There are no coincidences, but this was a confusing day. I was excited about the invitation but scared about the loss of the job. It had concerned me when I got a call from my boss for a late meeting that day. I called my prayer warrior, Bonnie and asked her to pray while I was in this meeting. The district had lost the money to pay for my position. What was the answer? God had been talking to me for a long time, and I know now I was not listening. That is why my work and health were suffering. That night I prayed. The answer I received was that God didn't want me to fight the fight to help parents and teachers anymore. I didn't have the support from the district that was needed. I was working too hard when God had other ideas for me. A lesson I learned was that there are lots of important courses, jobs, nonprofits, and ways to spend your time but is it the one God needs you for. That will be the one that is best for you and the world.

The summer before I had been feeling uneasy and set up meetings with my pastor to help me understand what was going on. We met three times. At the second, meeting he gave me the book, The Hiding Place, by Corrie Ten Boom. As I read it, I remembered this small voice saying, "You need to write". After reading this book suddenly I knew how to write a book about my grief, but I still questioned my ability. When Pastor and I met, we talked a short time and the pastor said, "it sounds like you know exactly what you are to do but you told God NO!" He was right.

So, I decided that night I would retire. I was mad because I wasn't ready to quit and didn't like how it happened. I was scared because I wasn't ready financially, sad about how my passion was not my passion anymore but energized when I realized I had a new passion helping others who are grieving.

A new chapter entered my life, everything was happening fast. I talked to my mom and sister about me moving out to the family farm in the shack in the back, so I could write, sell my house and save money. I invited friends to help me understand the project because this would be out of my knowledge base and comfort zone. One friend said instead of spending money on that shack you should take care of the big house. It didn't take long for me to realize that the shack would take a lot more work and money than I wanted to put in it. Most of the family thought I was crazy, and they were glad when I changed direction.

Ideas, possibilities, decisions, and actions were happening so fast. I sold my house and moved in with my mom while we worked on the big family house. We were just going to do what had to be done, foundation, new plumbing and electricity and painting the outside. You see this was a historic home that was built by my great grandfather in 1903. It was 110 years old and family had lived in it for all those years expect the last 3 years. This was a lot bigger job than what the shack would have been. I definitely wasn't prepared.

Now, remember how I worried about retirement funds? That hadn't changed but I had my house ready to sell and then it didn't. In my plan I would sell it, make money and save money as we worked on the project. I now realize that the six months I didn't sell my house made me have to deal with a bad habit I had developed since Garry's death. Before Garry died, I never worried about money. I never wanted for anything, but I didn't want that much. I didn't spend much money except at Christmas time. Since Garry had died, I had spent a lot of money. With nothing to show for it much; I gave to nonprofits, I paid for people's meals a lot because I thought I was such bad company, I would pay for them to eat with me (this was all in my mind). Trying to figure who I was and what I liked; I would just buy what I liked, not concerned about what I was spending. When the house didn't sell, I got in a fix. So, I had to step back and take action. I signed up for the Dave Ramsey Financial Peace University. It was important and became more important as the project went forward. You will find out why soon.

I put my house on the market in August 2013. I started the work on the family home about the same time. I got bids and contractors to work on the project. (Which remember was to take care of what needed to be done.) We started with the foundation in November 2013. In January the contractors showed up and things really moved. I moved out of my house in March 2014 and lived with my mom until July 2015.

During this time, I was on the ride of my life. I was making decisions and my schedule was busy. Life was busy but exciting, I felt so alive and working within my passion again. I felt like I was Moses. God does not call the equipped; he equips the called. I was in the middle of a project that if I knew what it would have turned out to be and cost, I would have said I could not do it. God knows us so well, our true heart's desires and how to support us if we call up on him. We started the project as planned and God sent wonderful craftsmen who uncovered original treasures of the house that changed and blessed this once simple project.

I must go back in time for a moment to share an event that later would affect the change in the project. In 2003 my mom put our family farm up for sale. It was hers and her decision. I had always loved the house and farm and when Garry and I came back to Texas, I thought one day we would have the house and farm and take care of my brother. So, when she signed the papers for the sale, it was like my dream would not come true. It upset me but I had to get over it. I prayed and asked God to help me let this go. He did; he gave me this message; "Debby I didn't put you on this earth to take care of a house. I have plans for you." This gave me peace even though I did not understand what God's plan was. As time continued, Garry died in 2006, I grieved, and the economic fall came in 2008, we did sale part of the farm. They pulled out of the buying the house and the rest of the farm.

Now, back to the project and the treasures we uncovered. We uncovered a beautiful arch in the main hall and the next day we uncovered a curved part of the staircase. All of this had been covered up when they added indoor plumbing in 1947. I didn't know any of it was there. The next day when

I walked in the hall and looked up at all we uncovered I realized God had presented me with a hidden treasure. This had always been grandma's house, but I didn't think about it as a beautiful and masterfully built house for its time. In that moment, the powerful memory of my saying God help me give this house up was reversed. I got goose bumps as I realized I was getting the house I always wanted, and that God had a plan far beyond what I could have imagined. The impact of that memory was not lost on me and gave a new purpose because in that moment I knew something special was at work here. So, for the next two years, I kept the project going. Now, it was not just "let's take care of what was needed" but "was to bring this house back to its glory" and the house was extraordinary. When I give tours of it now, I am still in awe that a simple project changed and turned out with no forethought and planning. It was orchestrated by God and competed under his direction.

Do you see the power in what happened there? I asked God to help me give up something special and when I did, he never forgot. He returned it in a way that was exciting, wonderful and had purpose for me and God.

I was growing, learning, and making decisions I never would have thought I could have done God was making me whole and my confidence was returning. This brings us to a second important point about the process. As the project changed so did the budget. During the project I made my payments and continued to stay current. If I had known how much the project would cost and the extent of renovations I would never have started. Remember when my house didn't sell, and I took the money course, now its truc impact was critical. It was necessary I understood money even though sometimes I took real risk. Only through prayer and discipline did it happen. Today, I continue to struggle with how to be responsible and live generously since all we have is God's and we are just stewards. It is all about living wisely and daily asking if you are on the right track. Sometimes you're not and then God sends help. Only prayer and a close relationship with God will let you know what is right for **you**. Others might disagree, but you must decide if you will live generously or afraid. God provides for what he wants to happen if we have the courage and discipline to stay close to God and listen to his lead. It is a true step of faith.

Now, with the house being competed, let's get back to the name sake of this chapter, The Breathe Retreat. I had time to spend on writing and getting back to the vision. It had never left my mind. The vision had not changed even though there would be a new location. We would have the Breathe Retreats at my home but now my home was a beautiful, peaceful and restful place on the top of a hill. The house has a spirit that people can feel. This house is not just about the beauty but about the love and service that has always been part of its history and will continue to lift people up. While the house was under construction, I had continued to volunteer and help the Christi Center. Now, was the time to move forward and make the Breathe Retreat a reality.

It was time to move, but I was stuck. I had the faulty assumption that if God had given me this plan, it was mine to complete. Having just finished this huge project of renovation and using my creative skills and collaborative skills to bring master craftsmen to understand my ideas and vision for the house I was ready. Why was I getting stuck in all the details for the Breathe Retreat? As I shared with a friend my dilemma, she said the ministry is to be shared and is not my ministry but God's. I needed to include others in the planning. That was all I needed. The words of wisdom from a fellow woman of God. Immediately, I knew what to do. I prayed for the ministry and watched for who God would send. I thought about women who I respected and impacted my life and had some connection to service and/or grief. I invited 15 women to serve as a prayer circle for this ministry, The Breath Retreats. We met at my home in July 2016. My idea was to share my vision and how I had nurtured it throughout the years. At the meeting I gave a history of the vision and how it stayed alive all these years. I read excerpts from my journal. I explained the broad concepts of the Breathe Retreat. They asked questions and with their help we came up with a plan for me to get started. We listed needs and suggestions and a list of those who would meet again to help plan the details for the Breathe Retreats. Then I could present to the staff of the Christi Center. Those attending and others continued to pray for the ministry as I worked with others.

For the next year, I met with small groups and the Christi Center. Finally, in June 2017 we planned the first Breathe Retreat to be held on Feb 18th, 2018. It was a success and the second one was scheduled and held in June that year. It had been a long road. It had taken 10 years for the vision that was conceived in 2008 to become a reality.

Saying "yes! to God" doesn't mean easy or quick. A closer walk with God has been a ride with highs and lows. God knows every part of me, my wishes, strengths, weaknesses, passions, sins, guilt and all I've been through. God guides me all the way. The good, the bad, and the ugly made my life rich and has transformed me into the woman I am today. Living a life following and asking for guidance allows me freedom and surprises and a life that is worth living.

SAY YES TO GOD AND ENJOY THE RIDE.

Debby Krueger

Debby is a woman who loves people and her life. She has had a little voice in her head for years saying, " You need to write." She has written personal journals, presentations for her passions and as a teacher taught little ones to find their voice in writing. Now, she has found her voice as she shares her life, the good, the bad, and the ugly as God walks with her. Read as this wife, mom, widow, teacher, and friend shares her journeys and life as God walks by her side.

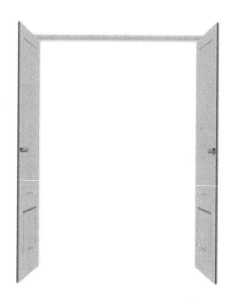

Holly Fenney
Yes, God!

Each of us has a journey that God has taken us on. Ther e are moments that occur along that journey that really helped to shape and define who we are. Share one of tho se Yes, God moments you have encountered, where you had to trust Him without knowing all the steps.

I contemplated how I wanted to start my chapter; how I wanted to start with my little piece of wisdom and contribution to share with women of all types, reading with great anticipation and expectancy of gathering tools to be stacked up in their own personal toolbox of life skills. In this toolbox of life skills, you might find collected words to use at your disposal such as faith, hope and love – especially if you are a Christian woman with scripture verses to whip out of your back pocket whenever you need to combat Satan and his troop of demons. And these are powerful words to have in your toolbox and should be used according to 1 Corinthians 13:13 where it states *'And now these three remain: faith, hope and love. But the greatest of these is love.'* (NIV); however, there is one word that God keeps pressing upon my heart, not only to keep in my toolbox, but to actually use it. I've tried to ignore it, pass it off and even question God on the validity and relevance, but it is crystal clear – vulnerability. There it is – in black and white – and we will explore this word through my story – through my vulnerability.

According to Merriam-Webster Dictionary, to be vulnerable is to be open for attack among other definitions. That specific definition is alarming. No one let me repeat, no one wants to be open for attack. God even talks about protecting ourselves against attacks in Ephesians 6:10-18 where it *states 'Finally, be strong in the Lord and in his mighty power. Put on the full armor of God, so that you can take your stand against the devil's schemes. For our struggle is not against flesh and blood, but against the rulers, against the authorities, against the powers of this dark world and against the spiritual forces of evil in the heavenly realms. Therefore, put on the full armor of God, so that when the day of evil comes, you may be able to stand your ground, and after you have done everything, to stand. Stand firm then, with the belt of truth buckled around your waist, with the breastplate of righteousness in place, and with your feet fitted with the readiness that comes from the gospel of peace. In addition to all this, take up the shield of faith, with which you can extinguish all the flaming arrows of the evil one. Take the helmet of salvation and the sword of the Spirit, which is the word of God. And pray in the Spirit on all occasions with all kinds of prayers and requests. With this in mind, be alert and always keep on praying for all the Lord's people.'* (NIV) God also says in Proverbs 4:23 to guard our hearts; it states, *'Above all else, guard your heart, for everything you do flows from it.'* (NIV) So, how in the world does vulnerability fit into the Word of God that emphasizes protection? Well, there are at least fifty verses in the Bible about vulnerability and we will explore some of them as we move forward. Yes, God shows us how to protect ourselves with the armor of God, but He also shows us that through vulnerability, it opens up an opportunity for grace to shine.

In 2 Corinthians 12:9-10, it states *'But he said to me, "My grace is sufficient for you, for my power is made perfect in weakness." Therefore, I will boast all the more gladly about my weaknesses, so that Christ's power may rest on me. That is why, for Christ's sake, I delight in weaknesses, in insults, in hardships, in persecutions, in difficulties. For when I am weak, then I am strong.'* (NIV)

My journey on the road to vulnerability is ongoing in both my personal and professional life, but I want to give you a snap shot into my professional life because it has been a difficult struggle for me to separate my identity from what I do to that of whom I really am; my true identity – which is in-Christ – daughter to the King Himself, God the Almighty.

It was August 2017 when I was approached by the operations manager of a well-respected and established local employment staff agency. She was excited and I could see in her eyes that she had something very important to tell me. She pulled me aside and asked if I would be interested in becoming her business partner as the owners were looking to sell. Before I even gave it serious thought, I blurted out, "Yes!" I recall even giving my answer with a little boogie dance. The idea of it was exciting and I had just come back from my day out pounding the pavement in my sales role with potential prospects; so, I was pumped up. I have to admit; the idea had already crossed my mind and I had a suspicion that the owners were getting ready to retire soon.

My job position was part recruiter and part sales and marketing. I moved into sales after the first few months on the job and thoroughly loved it. In fact, I was told later that the current partner who ran the business on the sales and marketing side recommended me to partner up with the operations manager to continue the business and its legacy.

To my surprise, the operations manager approached me before she knew that information. It appeared it was the right path and all the signs were pointing that God orchestrated this so-called happy ending – or beginning to an amazing career as a business owner.

What a compliment – Wow! Little 'ol me who came from nothing except the school of hard knocks and who learned how to pull her boot straps up and get 'r done with limited support - had the opportunity of a lifetime. It seemed too good to be true, but I knew my God was big and I banked on this opportunity as a blessing straight from Him. Before I continue on the path of business ownership, I think it is important that I back up and share what led me to this great opportunity of a lifetime.

My battle with identity has followed me since the day I was born. I am an identical twin. When I tell people that I am an identical twin, their eyes light up and say something to the effect of, "Oh, I wish I had a twin!" They are so excited and want to hear the glamour and fun of being a twin - and there are some. I love my twin sister; however, no one wants to hear the hardship of being a twin, especially if you are an identical twin. From the outside looking in, they see a picture-perfect friendship that supports one another with an inseparable bond. The bond is real but mix that with a dysfunctional family and there is serious trouble brewing.

Coming from a broken home where there was verbal and emotional abuse, and some physical abuse, the demands put on myself and my siblings shifted our relationships and how we related to each other. We were in survival mode – and in survival mode – survival of the fittest applied. So, I became the peacemaker and my identity was defined in the shadow of my twin sister who was the aggressor of the two of us. It was my place and I settled in until I was forced to become comfortable with the reality of my new wardrobe. It became the identity I would carry with me up until my mid-forties – even though I was a born-again Christian who was saved and baptized with the Holy Spirit living in me – and had a new identity in Christ since my mid-twenties. The baggage of my former identity stuck for so many years for many reasons. One being that it is common for people to compare twins; it's natural, which made it far more difficult to break away into who God made me – aside from my twin sister.

Still, I tried. And I tried. And I tried. What I discovered in all of my "trying" is that I simply needed to step into my new identity. It was a gift God had already given me, but I needed to believe it, embrace it and walk in it. Sounds easy, doesn't it? It wasn't. It takes intention, practice and determination to sever unhealthy patterns that are woven into the tapestry of the soul.

In Philippians 2:12, it states *'So then, my dear ones, just as you have always obeyed [my instructions with enthusiasm], not only in my presence, but now much more in my absence, continue to work out your salvation [that is, cultivate it, bring it to full effect, actively pursue spiritual maturity] with awe-inspired fear and trembling [using serious caution and critical self-evaluation to avoid anything that might offend God or discredit the name of Christ].'* (AMP)

We have two natures. The old and the new; the flesh and the spirit. In 2 Corinthians 5:17, it states *'This means that anyone who belongs to Christ has become a new person. The old life is gone; a new life has begun!'* (NLT)

The choice is ours, daily. To work out our salvation does not mean we have to prove ourselves in our works to be saved. No, we are saved by the grace of God and the work Jesus already accomplished as it states in Ephesians 2:8-9 *'For by grace you have been saved through faith, and that not of yourselves; it is the gift of God, not of works, lest anyone should boast.'* (NKJV)

To work out our salvation is the continuation of our faith walk and to choose our new identity fully, completely and with confidence, knowing that the war has been won and that God will meet us where we are at today to help us walk through our battles in life. We are, my dear sisters-in-Christ, in the battle of two worlds with one foot on earth and the other in heaven. It is not easy, and we so desperately need to embrace our new identity in-Christ to experience the victory in store for us, not only in heaven, but on earth until we meet our final destination in heaven - home. The power does not come from us, but the One whom is in us – Christ Jesus.

So, there I was with a lifetime opportunity in one hand and my broken identity in the other. Because my identity in-Christ had not been developed strong enough, my new identity became my position at work. It became my self-worth and value. According to Gettysburg College, one third of our lives is spent in the workplace. That is a tremendous amount of time. Think about that for one moment. It's as much time as we spend in our waking hours in our homes and sometimes more. I had become an expert in people pleasing and overachieving to prove myself in the perfect identity I had created for myself. Maybe this doesn't happen to you, but as I write, it is making me uncomfortable - so much so that my skin is crawling. I don't want to be vulnerable. I don't want others to see my mistakes and shortcomings. I don't want to be... an outcast, judged, alone, and unpopular; however, that is where God has placed me. Why? That seems brutally cruel. That is, until you put it into context. As a new creature in Christ, we were made to be set apart; not to blend into the rat race of the world.

In Romans 8:30-39, it states 'God knew what he was doing from the very beginning. He decided from the outset to shape the lives of those who love him along the same lines as the life of his Son. The Son stands first in the line of humanity he restored. We see the original and intended shape of our lives there in him. After God made that decision of what his children should be like, he followed it up by calling people by name. After he called them by name, he set them on a solid basis with himself. And then, after getting them established, he stayed with them to the end, gloriously completing what he had begun. So, what do you think? With God on our side like this, how can we lose? If God didn't hesitate to put everything on the line for us, embracing our condition and exposing himself to the worst by sending his own Son, is there anything else he wouldn't gladly and freely do for us? And who would dare tangle with God by messing with one of God's chosen? Who would dare even to point a finger? The One who died for us—who was raised to life for us!—is in the presence of God at this very moment sticking up for us. Do you think anyone is going to be able to drive a wedge between us and Christ's love for us? There is no way! Not trouble, not hard times, not hatred, not hunger, not homelessness, not bullying threats, not backstabbing, not even the worst sins listed in Scripture: They kill us in cold blood because they hate you. We're sitting ducks; they pick us off one by one.

None of this fazes us because Jesus loves us. I'm absolutely convinced that nothing—nothing living or dead, angelic or demonic, today or tomorrow, high or low, thinkable or unthinkable—absolutely nothing can get between us and God's love because of the way that Jesus our Master has embraced us.' (MSG)

I think the point God is trying to drive home is this: He is with us, He is loving us, He is protecting us, and He is all the identity we need. And He desperately needs us to walk in that to show the world who He really is. We are set apart because we live by different practices. We live by different principles that are purposed to shape the God in us. Blending is popular - and the exact opposite of what Jesus did while He completed His ministry and mission on earth. He was vulnerable by obedience and by choice to show God's divine power and love to the world.

After what I thought was my destiny, my husband arranged a meeting with an attorney to get the show on the road and make this business deal happen. That was just the beginning and I had hope, but I also had absolutely no experience whatsoever in something as stout as a business deal and all the finite details that needed to be done. Thankfully, I was covered in prayer by a couple of my close friends and some family members.

My husband and I walked into the prestigious law firm for our appointment. I noticed the large bold logo sign perfectly designed and centered behind the receptionist desk. Although the receptionist warmly offered hot coffee or refreshing sparkling water while we waited, the professional décor screamed that I was no longer in Kansas (and Toto was nowhere to be found). I squirmed as I sat down and glanced at my husband, thinking about what he had said to me when I first told him about the news of the offer to become a business co-owner.

"You're playing with the 'Big Dogs' now." I was both exhilarated and terrified at the same time. I felt out of my league and yet, I felt as though God had opened this door and would equip me for what I needed to become a business owner. The first step was to get the advice of an experienced attorney that saw similar cases come across her desk day-in and day-out.

"Emily will be right with you," the receptionist reassured as she pushed her Gucci black framed glasses up and smiled with lips painted apple red (Emily was not the attorney's real name, but for discretion purposes, I will call her Emily).

After we were seated in the lobby, the door to the back offices swung open, exposing a confident and friendly woman eager to meet me. Emily was pleasant, intelligent, assertive, and knew her profession – very well. My husband enlightened me with regard to her skillset in preparation of our meet and greet consultation.

"She doesn't just bark. She bites," said my husband with assurance. This statement came straight from a trusted friend of my husband who had hired Emily to protect his sole proprietor business in the Information Technology field. That was what I needed. I needed someone who would be an advocate for me and to protect me financially with sound direction and years of experience to back it up. Emily led us to a conference room that had a large mahogany oval table ready and willing to sit ten around it. I sunk in one of the comfortable swivel leather chairs with high expectations.

Emily carefully dissected each piece of information I gave her and then went over a list. The list started with due diligence of identifying and exposing every square inch of the business from the operations agreement to the business plan to the non-compete employment agreement, to the..., well, you name it; it was on the list.

My high expectations drained to reality and planted disappointment right on my face. Due to my obligation of confidentiality, I am bound contractually not to disclose any financial information or other additional information about the staff company opportunity that was offered to me for purchase – other than to share that the more I researched, the more that I learned that it was not the right fit for me.

My potential business partner and I spent the next six months going round and round with numbers, facts, and professionals in the legal and financial industries – only to confirm one thing – the selling price was not in our best interest. We tried. And we tried. And we tried (boy, was this scenario familiar), but the sellers did not budge. Their twenty-plus years of blood, sweat and tears invested in their business were no doubt equated in their valuation and they wanted every - single – penny of what they were asking for. I could not fault them for that, especially after we were informed by legal representation that it is actually very frequent for business owners to include emotional value in their selling price. This was their baby built from scratch over a simple conversation and a brilliant idea that had been discovered while sitting at a kitchen table.

Still, the reality and the doubt circled me like a dark cloud; it got thicker as more time passed. God, what is going on? Why is this happening – and why in the world would something like this be offered only to be crushed by mere numbers? Am I not worthy of this opportunity? Am I not… this… am I not that? The downward spiral spun out of control reminding me of all that I am not. Oh yes, the devil was having a heyday with me! I was confused, but in 1 Corinthians 14:33, it states *'For God is not the author of confusion but of peace, as in all the churches of the saints.'* (NKJV)

The test and trials were set before me and just as promised in James 1:3, it states *'Be assured that the testing of your faith [through experience] produces endurance [leading to spiritual maturity, and inner peace].'* (AMP); the experience I was going through was growing my faith and developing my spiritual maturity and inner peace that led to confidence in God that He is my rock and knows what He is doing in my life as in Jeremiah 29:11, it states *"For I know the plans I have for you," declares the Lord, "plans to prosper you and not harm you, plans to give you a hope and a future."* (NIV)

For this, I am truly and eternally grateful. Beloved, fully trusting God was and is the best decision I have ever made. His Word (the Holy Bible) is truth in its entirety given as a gift to rest in peace and the promises of God regardless of outside circumstances. In John 16:33, Jesus says, *"I have told you these things, so that in me, you may have peace. In this world you will have trouble. But take heart! I have overcome the world."* (NIV) How did you develop your faith when it seemed like nothing was going right in your life? Share a situation where you had to develop your faith walk.

In 2 Timothy 1:7, it says *'For God has not given us a spirit of fear, but of power and of love and of a sound mind.'* (NKJV) I love that because it assures me that although I struggled with my identity and value internally, God promises that I have power, love and a sound mind through the Holy Spirit inside of me. I was so wrapped up in the lies of the enemy, believing that I was not worthy of such an opportunity. When in all truth, God was using this "opportunity" to separate my "who from my do". He was working on producing more fruit in me by breaking off old carnal (flesh) identity that clothed me in a false sense of worth and value. What a curve ball and a serious game changer!

Think of it this way, would you let your child have free reign in a candy store? Let me illustrate the scene. You are walking hand-in-hand with your five-year-old child who happens to target the picture of a large dangling peppermint candy cane that is half dipped in milk chocolate on a door that is draped in holiday lights (of course, it is Christmas time because that it is my favorite holiday and time of year).

The lights invite you into a candy store with barrels and barrels of every type of candy rich with flavor and fun. Now, let go of your child's hand. What would they do? Would they want anything and everything? They would most likely overfill and eat themselves silly until they became sick to their stomachs. Hence, this is my point.

The business opportunity was the candy store and I was the child who wanted anything and everything (to prove my value and worthiness through a title I would have attached myself to that would have further progressed my detachment to my true identity in-Christ). God loved me enough to say, "No, I am teaching you something." Did this mean God did not love me? Quite the contrary. Just as we love our children enough to give them their desires, we teach them first.

My youngest son is fifteen years old. I would be foolish to hand him the keys to my car and let him drive off without making sure he took a driver training class, had a lot of practice and passed his driver's test. It would be in his best interest. As a parent, that is responsible, loving and providing protection. And so, our heavenly father is with His children. Similar, God showed me the wisdom of walking away from the business opportunity and that it had nothing to do with my identity, worthiness or value – although every fiber in me felt like I had failed.

How did you stay motivated in a season where patience, faith and trust had to be exercised? Dealing with the loss of my expectations and moving into a different profession that led me back to my roots in the insurance industry, was wearing on my soul and I suffered anxiety that resulted in physical illness for several months. Detaching my being (my soul – which is my mind, body and emotions) from my situation and identity was one of the most challenging experiences God has brought me through to date. It was the biggest mountain I have had to climb, but it was necessary to bring healing to my identity.

In the Bible, it tells us that Jesus is a carpenter by trade. It was custom for fathers to teach their sons starting at the age of twelve. Joseph, Jesus' earthly-father, would have carried out this deed and certainly did; however, there is only one account in the gospels of Jesus being a carpenter.

In Mark 6:3, it states *'Is this not the carpenter, the son of Mary, and the brother of James and Joses and Judas and Simon? Are His sisters not here with us?" And they were [deeply] offended by Him [and their disapproval blinded them to the fact that He was anointed by God as the Messiah].'* (AMP)

I find it very interesting that people discounted Jesus as being anointed by God as the Messiah merely because of His profession. Perhaps it was too practical for them. Jesus was a carpenter and most likely used the practicality of a builder profession for His many parable lessons to teach about the spiritual realm.

The fact is that Jesus breathed, lived, and learned on earth just as we do every day. He was human; however, we know more about his three-year tenure in ministry than anything else. Why? Because that was His purpose. He was set apart to change the world and to teach the world about God's love for humanity. Similar, we are called to continue the legacy of Jesus as His disciples and separate our performance and profession (practicality) from our purpose and mission (spirituality).

Once I understood this truth – really wrapped my brain around this concept - something clicked inside of me. Everything changed for me; my outlook on life had been renewed. It reminds me of the famous hymn "Turn Your Eyes Upon Jesus" written by Helen Howarth Lemmel in the early 1900s:

"Turn your eyes upon Jesus,
Look full in His wonderful face.
And the things of earth will grow strangely dim,
In the light of His glory and grace!"

The things of earth become strangely dim compared to the glory of Jesus – very dim. My revelation of this helped keep me focused and motivated when I did not see where God was taking me on my personal path with Him.

I also had to learn about boundaries and implement them. It was necessary. It was necessary in my professional life and my personal life. Boundaries allowed me to be vulnerable (so that I would walk in being set apart) yet protected me at the same time.

Relying on the truth of God's Word was vital to my endurance in this season of change for me. I discovered that to be able to move forward with child-like vulnerability – yet with purpose and protection – the Word of God had to be my bread of life.

What scriptures, books or resources do you recommend using when you are looking to grow in your walk with God?

There are many biblical promises from God that have helped me with my faith to grow and trust in Jesus.

Here are a few:

'And we know that God causes everything to work together for the good of those who love God and are called according to his purpose for them.' Romans 8:28 (NLT)

'It is better to trust in the Lord than to put confidence in man.' Psalms 118:8 (KJV)

'No weapon that is formed against thee shall prosper; and every tongue that shall rise against thee in judgment thou shalt condemn. This is the heritage of the servants of the Lord, and their righteousness is of me, saith the Lord.' Isaiah 54:17 (KJV)

'Fear not, for I am with you; be not dismayed, for I am your God; I will strengthen you, I will help you, I will uphold you with my righteous right hand.' Isaiah 41:10 (ESV)

There are so many amazing resources available to grow in our Christian love walk; here are a few that have strengthened me and may be of interest to you:

New York Times Bestseller, Boundaries, *When to Say Yes - How to Say No - to Take Control of Your Life (and set healthy, biblical boundaries)* – written by Dr. Henry Cloud and Dr. John Townsend

Pastor Rick Warren – Daily Devotional Hope (PastorRick.com). This resource has been a wonderful lifeline for me as I listen to it every morning as I get ready to start my day. It is just enough to get me fed spiritually daily and is approximately twenty minutes.

K-Love, Positive and Encouraging Radio Station (klove.com). I listen to this radio station in my car when I commute to and from work – or whenever I can. It lifts my spirit and puts my focus in perspective to what matters – loving people and worshiping God.

With these resources, I have sought medical treatment for my past abuse and anxiety mentioned in this chapter. Jesus continues to heal me through both His Word and physically through medical professionals. I would encourage anyone suffering from abuse, depression and/or anxiety to seek help for wellness.

In 3 John 1:2 it states *'Beloved, I pray that in every way you may succeed and prosper and be in good health [physically], just as [I know] your soul prospers [spiritually].'* (AMP)

Holly Fenney

Holly Rae Feeney is a two-time author, sharing her passion to inspire others of the love of God through her writing. Her first book, *His Spirit Stands - Inspired by a True Story of Triumph over Tragedy*, was published by UImpact Publishing in December 2015.

In March 2018, Holly made the difficult decision to leave her job position in the staffing/recruiting industry and return to her roots in the insurance industry, re-obtaining her licensure in Property/Casualty and Life/Health. She is currently pursuing her Certified Insurance Service Representative (CISR) designation and is very active as a founding member of a developing Business Networking International Chapter located in Oro Valley, AZ that will launch in 2019.

Holly enjoys her volunteer position with a non-profit organization, Hands of Hope, formally known as Crisis Pregnancy Center that practices and promotes Biblical principles in providing support to women facing unplanned pregnancies; the same organization that came to Holly's assistance in 1995 when she unexpectedly became pregnant with her first son which let her to give her life to Jesus Christ as her Savior.

Holly and her husband, Troy, have been married for 17 years and reside in Tucson, AZ with their children of a blended family, Brandon (23), Jessie (21), Savannah (19), and Aaron (15). Their family continues to be blessed and grow with the addition of Kassandra, their daughter-in-law, and three grandchildren – McKenna Mae (2), Hayden James (1) and Jameson Dean (6 months) – that keep them young at heart and overjoyed with love!

Valena Spradley
Yes, God!

Each of us has a journey that God has taken us on. There are moments that occur along that journey that helped to shape and define who we are. Share one of those Yes, God moments you have encountered, where you had to trust Him without knowing all the steps.

My first thought when I asked to participate in this project was "But I'm not a good enough Christian. I don't read my bible every day, I lose my temper with my family, I love Jesus, but I cuss a little…." There are so many reasons why I am not a good example. I wondered "Why would anyone want to hear my story?". Then God said, "Do this". It wasn't an audible voice – I've learned that when God speaks it is quiet…it is a still voice – a nudge, a calming of my spirit. I decided to go for it and see where this path leads me and hopefully you can find something to help and encourage your journey. So, this now becomes another Yes, God moment for me.

One example of saying Yes, God and trusting was 19 years ago. I had just gotten divorced – for the second time. First, let me say that no one ever gets married thinking they will be divorced. You have all the hopes and dreams of a family, a partner and a great photo for the Christmas card. But sometimes divorce happens. You survive, you heal, you hope you haven't damaged your children while you save yourself. Then you struggle as a single mom, meet a nice guy at church and think "Hey, maybe I can make this work!" You build a house together – write all the bible verses on the studs, show up at church every time the doors are open but 3 years later find yourself even further away from God and away from your true self. I found myself divorced again. Being twice divorced in a small town is a very hard thing to overcome. I had church members who prayed with me to help my marriage but once that marriage ended, they wouldn't speak to me at the mall. I pulled away from God and away from everyone because I was a failure. What was wrong with me? Why can't I choose the right one? Did I not listen correctly to God's voice? Then I went back to my former church. I found a Sunday School class with a teacher who showed God's love in ways I had never seen. She invited me to a weekly lunchtime bible study. It was there that I grew and studied and found out more about God's love than I had ever been taught before. This group of ladies did not judge me – they didn't treat me like the failure that I saw every time I looked in the mirror.

My son was in high school and had picked out his college. I decided I was done with the small-town life and it was time to follow him to the city. I started job hunting – even landed an interview. But God had a different plan for my life. While attending this fabulous Sunday School class – which ironically was a group of married folks – some newlyweds, some with littles and some with teenagers our teacher Miss Joy saw a man visiting church for the first time and invited him to join us. He – like me – had grown up in the Baptist Church in the Dallas area. He had moved to our town to get away from city life and his parents had retired here. He was trying to find a church and had visited our Methodist one. He joined our class; the church also had a small singles group that met occasionally. I was not looking for a husband – I was not even looking for a date! At this point I was 35 years old focusing on being a good mom, trying to change my life and career and learning more about God's love. I didn't have time for a relationship. But God had Kyle picked out for me – for us. We began dating, grew together spiritually and were married in 2000. I remember my prayers during this time. "God, I know you have a plan for me I know my life has already been mapped out, but could you please just show me a corner of the map, so I know where I am headed." I kept my heart and my eyes focused on the future – sometimes Yes, God is a long waiting game.

How did you develop your faith when it seemed like nothing was going right in your life? Share a situation where you had to develop your faith walk.

The last year of my life has been the most challenging both personally and professionally. Four years ago, I was hired as Vice President of Business Development for a community bank building a new branch in our small town. I have been in Bank Marketing for over 20 years and this was a fantastic opportunity with a nice promotion. On January 4th of 2017 my boss told me she had good news for me – they were changing my job and I would now be a loan officer. This was not a position that I have ever wanted. I love being a community representative, coordinating events, finding customers and introducing them to a loan officer and then helping them with other business products. Looking at credit reports, analyzing tax returns, learning to read CAD reports and telling people no they are not credit worthy was the exact opposite of my core personality.

During this time my parent's health declined rapidly and I became their driver and care giver. My mom is fighting Alzheimer's and my dad has COPD and is diabetic. Visits to the ER have become routine. There was one day I will never forget, I was at a business luncheon and my mom called saying my dad had a high fever and wasn't breathing. I rushed to their house as the ambulance pulled up. My mom was very upset and very confused. I helped her out of her pajamas, found her shoes, purse and house keys and we headed to the hospital. When we arrived at the hospital mom began having a panic attack and they admitted her as well. I was running between the two rooms and at one point stopped a nurse and said, "I need you to pat me on the head and tell me I can do this." That sweet young man did exactly that. During the next year I frequently saw him in the halls, and he would always give me a thumbs up. Dad spent 2 weeks in the hospital a couple of weeks in rehab and then was released to go home. I was able to get some assistance for them and we settled into a routine. But then 3 months later my husband was diagnosed with kidney disease. We discovered he only has one functioning kidney and it had several large stones. After 2 trips to the ER and 4 unsuccessful procedures to break up the stones, he was sent to Houston. Where he underwent a 5-hour surgery to remove the stones the week before Christmas and then another surgery a few months later on his thyroid to stop the kidney stones from forming.

There was one Friday night when my mom called saying she needed to go to the ER and the conversation went like this…. "Mom, please dial 911. I cannot take you right now because I am taking Olivia to her first band performance and

Kyle is already in the ER so I will meet you at the hospital."
She was having another panic attack and my husband
another kidney stone attack… Looking to God kept me on
track, kept me focused. When your world becomes so
narrow you have to rely on prayer. I believe God heard my
cry for help and calmed my spirit. He sent me friends who
texted "What can I do" and my first thought was I need
Chick Fil A and she showed up at the ER with Chick Fil A.
I also reached out to a friend when I needed to deliver school
fund raising items that we had sold. "Susan, can you come
to my house and sort these orders and deliver them for me?"
She didn't hesitate, the popcorn was delivered, and she got
the blessing of being able to help someone in need.

You know we all have times in our lives where our home
life is stressful – health issues, marriage struggles or life with
teenagers. And then we go thru seasons of work stress –
burn out, too many demanding projects, difficult co-workers
but usually during these times you can escape one of these
situations. You focus on work when your home life is
stressful, you decompress at home each night to escape the
work stress. But when you are in a place where there is no
rest it becomes so very hard to keep on your happy face. I
became a robot – one foot in front of the other. Survival,
keep smiling, take care of everyone was my daily routine. I
lied to everyone – my boss would ask "How are you coming
along?" "I'm doing great – learning so much!" My daughter
would ask "Mom, is work getting better?" "Yes, baby I'm
learning a lot." My husband "How was work?" "Good, I
didn't cry today." My parents, "Thank you so much for all
that you do for us. How's your job?" "It's great and it's
really no trouble at all." But late at night and early in the

mornings I would cry to God. "Please give me the strength to handle all of these things. Good wife, mom and daughter, employee, Christian, caregiver to so many, and friend." I had to plan my time with God and my time alone.

During the last two years I've taken trips away - all by myself. I first went to the Texas Hill Country in the Spring to see the beauty wild flowers. I was gone for 4 days. It was the first time I had traveling alone that didn't involve work. Stepping out of your normal routine, stepping out alone and more importantly to me – stepping out into nature gave me the time to focus on God and get myself back to center. When we have so many voices pulling us in different directions , we can't hear that still calm voice of God showing us the way.

How did you stay motivated in a season where patience, faith and trust had to be exercised?

As I talked about in the last question this current season of my life has been trying on every level. I have stayed motivated by learning to lean on others and sharing my struggles. Thankfully my husband's health has improved - it's been a struggle for all of the family limiting red meat, but everyone is now healthier.

It has been several months since my parents were in the hospital. I take them to their doctor appointments and have found social services to help them with tasks like grocery shopping and house cleaning. If you are caring for the elderly, please check to see what social services are available to help them – and you. I found the hardest task for me was grocery shopping on Saturday's. Mom's list is hard to decipher when milk is listed 4 times and on 3 separate pages. I was also purchasing groceries for my family – which often got thrown away because who has the time or the energy to cook a healthy meal when you are under this much stress? If I only had a dollar for every bag of kale or piece of fruit, I've thrown away I would have Olivia's college tuition taken care of. I cannot tell you the relief it is now that someone else does the grocery shopping for my parents. I think we stay motivated by the little wins - the little steps that lift just one of those heavy stones from our shoulders.

While the health of my family stabilized the stress of my job increased. I was given production goals and was becoming increasing overwhelmed with the work required . Crying in the bathroom at work became a regular occurrence. I began seeking other employment. I have been very blessed during my work career. I have had career success and when I've applied for a new position I've usually been hired. Two of my former jobs were created after I spoke to the Bank President and told them they should hire me as their Marketing Director and listed my skill set. My last job they came to me, sought me out for my particular skill set and hired me.

When that situation changed it was surprising and hurtful, but I thought "I'll just go find another great job. Maybe it's time for a career change. This last year I've learned about tax returns and bank requirements so now I can help others when they need a loan". I applied for a job in our area. Then a non-profit opportunity became available and I thought "This is it!". I was so excited... I polished up my resume to reflect non-profit volunteer work I had done, secured several letters of recommendation from prominent community leaders, and scheduled an appointment with the President. I hadn't been this excited in years. But I didn't read the requirements correctly and it stated bachelor's degree required - I do not have a college degree. One of my friends said, "Are you sure a degree isn't a requirement?", but I thought even if it is, I can overcome that.

Look I've got all these great references, I want to help people, God has helped me get every other job, he allowed me to struggle this last year to learn new skills to prepare me for this moment! I was so pumped.... Then I spoke again to the President and he told me he was sorry, but the degree was required not just preferred. I was devastated. How can this not be God's plan? I had been praying so hard, "Lord, please show me where you want me, Lord, I want to serve you and help others." I took a sick day, binged some Netflix, put on that happy face and went back to a job I hated more and more each day. When you are in a dark tunnel you know what you need, you need to focus on the positive, you need to eat healthy, exercise, meditate and find ways to relieve the stress. But it is easier to eat the chocolate, drink the wine, waste hours on Facebook. I did not spend enough time with God, but I did reach out to a small group of trusting friends asking for prayer and encouragement. Sometimes we become so weary that we can't even seem to pray for ourselves, and friends that is when we need to reach out and ask for help. I know without a doubt these friends that lifted me up keep me from staying in that dark tunnel.

But my rejection was not over. I dusted off my hurt ego, put those big girl panties on and applied for another non-profit job. This one was even better, helping women finish their education. Teaching them job skills, and how to provide for their family. Who could be a better leader than a woman who had been a single mom, who had worked her way up from menial jobs to being a VP at a bank? Okay so I took a hit with the last job I applied for but that just meant that this was the victory that awaited me! During a business lunch I happened to be sitting at the table with the board president of the organization. I told her I heard they were looking for a new director and I interested. Her face lit up, she hugged me and said was the best news she had heard all day. I sent her my resume, reached out to board members who like wise encouraged me to apply and was very happy planning my new career. I had such confidence, I had such hope, this was it. God was taking his time and making me wait, what a great story this would make for sharing. I dreamed about the things I would do and people I would help. A day later a board member emailed me the job description. And there at the top it said those words... Bachelor Degree Required. Not preferred - but required. I called the president and asked if that was truly a requirement and she said yes and apologized and said, "I'm so sorry, I didn't know you didn't have a degree." As I am typing this the tears and emotion have hit me once again. This is a fresh wound. It has been less than three months. All I heard in those words were failure... I didn't go to college, I failed in marriage, I am not good enough to help these women and most of all I failed in seeing God's plan for me.

How could I have been so cocky, so self-assured that I knew His plan for me? This devastation was a much harder blow to recover from. I took a sick day. This time I didn't watch TV, I didn't eat chocolate. I sat and cried out to God, "What have I done wrong? I was trying to help people, I was willing to take a huge pay cut and walk away from the corner office, the title and all of the trappings of success. Am I not good enough?" All of the failures in my life kept coming back to me, you failed at two marriages – never mind I've been happily married for 18 years, you failed because you didn't go to college – never mind the VP title and good salary, you failed at two job positions that were helping people – never mind the years of community service and happiness I've had serving others.

The devil is so good at kicking us when we are down. Every negative thought and many I had never thought of were hurled at me, in my mind. My husband and friends were telling me all of the positive things about me and this situation , but I couldn't hear them over the yelling in my head. I reached out to one particular friend after it was suggested that if I wanted to work in with a nonprofit perhaps, I should finish my degree. Well folks I never even started my degree and I have a daughter who will start college in two years. How could I afford to do that? My friend asked if I wanted to pursue a degree, I thought for a moment and said no. She laughed, offered to give me one of her degrees and she said, "Figure out what you want to do and do it." Such simple difficult words. And then I thought of my favorite bible verse. Psalms 46:10 "Be still and know that I am God". I have never felt that God has abandoned me, but I have felt his silence.

I sat in my closet, I'm very lucky I have a big closet that until 2 years ago had a desk built along the back wall. I asked my contractor husband to tear out the desk and build me a book case. I purchased a chair from a friend, painted the wall a soothing blue and grey and now have my perfect prayer, runaway and hide space in my home. It has a large window that I am looking out right now as the beautiful fall leaves tumble to the ground and the birds eat from the feeder outside. I became still, I didn't cry. I have shed so many tears of stress, sadness and frustration in the last year I don't have many left. I sat quietly and then an idea came to my mind. What if I quit my job? My husband had been self-employed for the last 6 years and had just gotten a new full-time job with great benefits, a complete answer to prayer. What if we switched roles? I could pursue my passion of photography and marketing and maybe even pursue that secret dream of being a writer? I could pick up my daughter from school, I could better care for my parents without the pressure of having to get back to work after each doctor appointment. I timidly brought the idea to my husband and he was willing to figure out a way to make it work.

This Yes, God was different. "Yes, God I will accept that you always have a plan for me, Yes, God I will not try to write the script for you. Yes, God I am humbled and so thankful to you for this new path." Six months ago, I never would have dreamed I could work from home, turn in those corporate keys or be asked to participate in a book writing project. All of these are because of Yes, God.

What scriptures, books or resources do you recommend using when you are looking to grow in your walk with God?

Earlier I shared that my favorite scripture has always been Psalms 46:10. Be still and know that I am God. A few years ago, our Sunday School class went thru one of Jen Hatmaker's earliest books, The Girlfriend's guide to Bible Study. She talked about really dissecting each word of a verse. Be.... This is good to simply Be. Be still... I think I can be still. Be still and know... This is deep. Be still and know that I am. Good old testament stuff here, I'm picturing Charlton Heston as Moses on the mountain. Be still and know that I am God. We know how much he loves us and how Jeremiah 29:11 says "For I Know The Plans I Have For You declares the Lord, Plans to Prosper You and Not to Harm You, Plans to Give You Hope and a Future.'"

I enjoy ladies who laugh while teaching you about the bible and how to stay on this chosen path. It has been so liberating to hear ladies like Jen Hatmaker speak so open and honestly about the struggles of being a Christian woman today. These women are not perfect, and they humbly share their struggles with humor. I have taken several Beth Moore bible studies over the years and she is so in depth and deep in the way she teaches you to study the word. My Christian influence has pivoted and changed in the last few years. , I have become more liberal in the way I see the world and see my place as a Christian. When Jesus was asked how to have eternal life, he answered, "You must love the Lord your God will all your heart, all your soul, your strength and your mind. And love your neighbor as yourself." Loving others around us is a vital step to becoming closer to God. And when we say Yes, God I will give of my time, give of my money to help others it's amazing how that helps you focus on the things that truly make an eternal difference. Another favorite verse that is Ecclesiastes 4:9 "Two people are better off than one, for they can help each other succeed."

I am learning how powerful the prayers of others can be. God has guided me this year and led me to a group of women that I never would have known if not for Him bringing our paths together. These ladies live 3 hours away from me. We are different in age, in religious background, some political issues, in marital status and in race yet the power when this group prays for each other is so profound. Thru the power of social media, we can pop onto our secret Facebook group and ask for specific prayer at the moment we need it. And it never fails when one of us post an urgent prayer it seems someone just happens to check their phone and sends an encouraging word. Prayer works and prayer partners are vital to survival. You need to find your tribe, pray for God to bring the people together than he wants together and then move out of his way, listen and follow the path that he will prepare for you.

I would also recommend stepping out of your comfort zone, try a different style of teacher. I recently read a book by Nadia Bolz-Weber "Accidental Saints – Finding God in all the Wrong People" It is a book about grace, about love and about real life, not just the perfectly starched Christian we think of who are in church every time the doors are open. This book is about saying Yes, God and seeing God in every person we encounter.

Valena Spradley

Valena Spradley started her career working at the Lufkin Daily News in the composing department as a proof runner – taking the ads to the customer for approval and making sure the changes were made properly. She watched the design and layout process and knew she wanted to create. She spent several years at a printing company, then an advertising agency hired her to create, design and work with clients. Valena has loved photography since high school and was able to use this talent at the ad agency. The agency closed – Valena opened her own agency and continued taking care of the clients. This led to the next step in her career when one of her clients – a local home town bank asked if she would be interested in coming to work for them as their Marketing Director. She continued in the Banking field for the next 22 years as a Marketing Director, Business Development Officer, and Lender.

"I love living in the small town of Lufkin, Texas", says Valena. "We are a close-knit community that will rally to help our neighbors and support each other." Valena is very involved in many civic organizations. She has served on several boards including The Junior League of Lufkin, Angelina Beautiful Clean, The Museum of East Texas, The Women's Networking Board, Leadership Lufkin Alumni, Main Street Lufkin, Leadership Tomorrow, The Salvation Army and her proudest community achievement – serving as President of the Lufkin Rotary Club. In 2018 she received the Role of Fame Award from Rotary for her many years of service.

Valena ended her banking career as a Vice President in 2018 to focus on her family and concentrate on her creative side. Thru the years she continued her photography– she loves archiving the perfect moment during family photos and capturing God's handiwork in nature. In October of 2018, she created Anchor V Innovations, LLC. Her company focuses on photography, graphic design, and marketing services. Valena says the best part of being your own boss is taking her daughter to school wearing yoga pants in the morning and getting to pick her up in the afternoon. Some of her favorite moments are spent at the beach so she incorporated the anchor into her company and logo.

Valena has been married to Kyle since 2000 and has two children. T.J., who is married to Morgan and has the cutest boys in the land. Thomas is 4 , Nolan is 2 and Nana V loves being able to spend more time with them. Her daughter Olivia – Livie- is a sophomore in high school and is a STEM girl, robotics queen, skeet shooter, 4 H member, and photographer.

She has learned the immeasurable value in time spent alone so you may see her on a country road in "Penelope" the grey Pathfinder. She's the one with the camera or iPhone trying to capture the magic light so she can then share that photo with her friends.

Her next goal is to start a blog – caregiver, mom, friend. All the things that make life stressful and beautiful at the same time.

Valena@AnchorVinnovations.com

Anchor V Photography on Facebook and Instagram

Kathy Daniel
Yes, God!

Each of us has a journey that God has taken us on. There are moments that occur along that journey that helped to shape and define who we are. Share one of those Yes, God moments you have encountered, where you had to trust Him without knowing all the steps.

Yes GOD! Two simple words and yet there is nothing simple about the "Yes" and nothing simple about the "GOD". I didn't realize what I was saying when I thought I was responding to God concerning different areas of my life. When the yes came to my heart and mind it was easy. When the actions surfaced that were necessary to move the "yes" forward, I froze and looked for a way out. My thoughts were, "Okay God, I said yes but maybe I should have reviewed the requirements of this new assignment before I said yes. I didn't know that the upcoming assignments would include some of my family members and some of my closest friends who knew me inside out and from "back in the day". The assignment was supposed to involve people that I didn't know and who didn't know me. You know what I'm saying; I did not want to be judged on my past nor did I want to appear as a hypocrite. I didn't know my journey would require me to pray every time a situation came up. And I didn't know I would have to give up some of my favorite habits and some so-called friends and places. I did not understand how much my conversation would change with people I was already talking to. To my surprise, I didn't mind the change because I knew I would need to talk to GOD more and more about what was going on and I was all for that". Somehow, though, I noticed how I had changed when I opened myself up to being obedient to God's will and to his way. My "Yes" developed a new character in me I didn't know existed. Slightly afraid of not knowing what to expect, I looked around to find somebody that could debate this thing with me, but I couldn't find "nobody. Nope, there was nobody. Just me and God! And like I said, what some people already knew about me was not pretty, loving, godly or kind. No one was there that I could trust to understand what I wanted to say or what I was going through or even could recognize that I had been given a new assignment for my life. OMG! Then suddenly, the things I KNEW ABOUT MYSELF crept into my mind and there I was, now paralyzed and discouraged by my past. NOW WHAT?

One of the hardest things that God had to get me to understand on this journey was that this journey was not even about me. He had to show me that the people he used to accomplish his will were people I'm sure would not have been chosen based on the standards in the world today. He reminded me through his word that Moses was uncertain of the responsibilities he was given. David was concerned only about himself until God redirected his motives. Saul started out as a Christian killer before his walk on the Damascus road where he became Paul. As did these leaders of God, it encouraged me to *bury my past, live in the present* and *embrace the future* with God on my side.

Growing up, I always thought that memories were intended to be pleasant, warm and comforting but I have discovered on this journey that memories can torment and trap you into a dark place. The devils' greatest weapon is to use our past against us. In one of the books I mentioned earlier, "The Blood" (Benny Hinn), the author shared these words:

So many people live in a never-ending cycle of hopelessness, despair, embarrassment, and failure because it is so difficult to forgive yourself and to bury the past. But thank the Lord that the moment the shed blood of Christ has been applied to your heart, your past is buried. It is gone forever, and no longer remembered in glory. Let these words sink into your heart.

I think I am a pretty sensitive person when it comes to talking with God. I cried profusely when I heard God say "Kathy, I love you and I have chosen you for this assignment. This is not an accident or coincident that you are at this stage in your life. I've been preparing you for such a time as this. Even you do not understand the changes that are taking place. You can handle it and I will be by your side the entire time. So, don't forget that "I AM" is here!" I cried more. I didn't see what God saw in me and I was scared. I was afraid. Fear step in and made me doubt what I was assigned to do. Have you ever been at a place in your life when you thought if I don't say it aloud then no one will hear about it and so it won't be true, or I don't have to respond? Well, it didn't matter if I spoke it out or not because the message was meant for me and I heard God. The message from God will be confirmed and confirmation from God is how the deal is sealed. Whatever God says, He will confirm. At this point, I was still a very new work in progress, and he was still working on me and what HE needed me to be.

So many times, have I wanted to quit the journey, but I did not want to disappoint God. My heart had changed. My mind and thoughts had been rearranged, and my walk and talk had been affected. So, if I quit, I thought nobody would know that I was being disobedient. YES, is not as simple as it sounds. I tried to justify why it shouldn't be me that the Lord needed to handle a given situation. I was just like the men and women used in the bible that felt like GOD should pick somebody else. So, the question was why me? But the bigger question was why not me? Why am I afraid? He said he would speak for me. He told me to decrease so that HE could increase in me. He promised He would never leave nor forsake me. I either believe or I don't. Move yourself out of the way.

One particular summer day, my husband and I took a road trip to Memphis to visit with some family members and to celebrate the graduation of our new doctor in the family. I wasn't sure that I wanted to go. I always have so many things to do and wanted to spend my time completing some of my open-ended projects.

Let me pause to give you a little history of my background. I am a graphic designer and was called to this profession by God. I was working in a bank as a supervisor of tellers and was over banking operations at a local branch. I had been in banking over 15 years but just wasn't quite comfortable regarding the outlook of my future. I knew I was stuck when I was not allowed to move into the Marketing department. I was told we were shorthanded, and no transfers were allowed. Yeah, okay! At that time, I was the only degreed person in the bank, and I was in hot pursuit of - studying to receive my Master of Business Administration degree. Even after that, I enrolled into graphic design classes at the Art Institute. My question was God why am I feeling this urgency to complete my education. It seems liked it was not connected. I know now that the more education you have the more opportunities you will have for growth. So, with all of this going on, I felt in my spirit that God wanted me to quit my current job so I could become more available for ministry. I was to start my business. Well I did so, even while family members where asking me what was wrong with me. To fast forward this story, many ministry opportunities opened for me even though we were now minus a paycheck in my home. Some hard times occurred, and my husband and I had to begin to trust and depend on God. Throughout this process, testimonies rose up in my household and the favor of God showed itself regularly within my small business, within new ministries and within new people that crossed my path. God was still working on me now more so than ever.

Okay, so here we are now faced with this trip to Memphis during the weekend and my Pastor encouraged me, as well as a few others that God had ministry there for me. I already knew I would miss church on Sunday. I dislike missing church, especially my church home services. I have such freedom and liberty in our worship service. I could not image how this would take place and how I would play a role or make a difference in the lives of my in-laws and their friends. So, we wake up on Sunday morning and gathered in the family den area. We each are having a cup of coffee and sharing small talk. My husband reaches to turn the television on, and somebody said, hey let's not turn on the television today. I knew that was God opening the door. So, I began with thanking God for all he had done in the lives of our family members. Others chimed in and gave God praise and then worship happened. A friend showed up from down the street, in much despair about how she has done everything she can to lead her sons to Christ so they could change their ways and live a better life. So, to encourage her heart, we shared scriptures and promises from the word of God, tears flowed, and prayer took its rightful place. As we stood to hold hands, to touch and agree that God is still on the throne, the Holy Spirit began to move from one person to the next. I raised my head to looked up and the size of the circle had grown. The number of people had increased. I was so grateful to God that I had moved out of the way while God blessed us and moved on the hearts of family and friends., Then, GOD was glorified. Everything always works out in His favor. The Word of God says,... We know that all things work together for good to them that love God, to them who are the called according to his purpose. (Romans 8:28) KJV.

How did you stay motivated in a season where patience, faith and trust had to be exercised?

I came upon some notes in a notebook in which I had written years ago in March 1992. I was journaling my thoughts with God. I didn't know what I was doing or if what I was doing made a difference in my life. I had done nothing like that before. But I guess back then, I thought it might be something that would organize my life and my commitment to God. There were two books I was reading. One of them was "The Blood" by Benny Hinn, and the other was "The Purpose Driven Life" by Rick Warren. In my reading, I came upon a prayer that was so powerful that I immediately wanted to be and do everything that was shared, and I didn't want to forget it, so I copied it into my notes and now is a good time to share it. It will cause me to examine myself and make me wonder if God had been looking at me the whole time with his arms crossed and thinking, she wrote it down, but she will forget she wrote it down but when the time is right, I will bring it back. Now here we sit in 2018, over 20 years ago that I found this prayer, and I faced what I asked for, what I promised, what I did and what I didn't do.

Here is the prayer;

Father I surrender to you now. I yield everything to YOU, my body, my soul, and my spirit, my family, my job, my finances, my weaknesses, my strengths, my past, my present, and my future, everything I am, for all eternity. I ask you Lord, to give me a repentant heart for all the things I've done to grieve you, all my sins, my iniquities, my coldness of heart, and my lack of trust. I ask you to empower me to turn around to go the other way, the way that pleases YOU. Holy Spirit I welcome you into my life right now. I praise you and love you. I ask you to help me received the things I've asked for from the Father through Jesus. Help me come into fellowship and communion with you, for I don't know how to do it by myself. Make me aware of your presence and enable me to hear your voice. I promised to obey. Lord Jesus anoint me with your Holy Spirit as I obey and learn. Give me power to touch those around me and those you will send across my path. Show me what to do next. And help me never to neglect your fellowship. I pray this in the name of Jesus my Lord and savior. Amen

Little did I know that God had taken notice of my prayer and placed it into his memory for me? I did not realize the assignments that God had for me had already begun. All of that stuff I was saying about yielding everything to God… boy did he ever. I have learned that when I pray for things like a job and finances, watch out, because things happen to your finances and to your job but not in the way you might imagine. When you pray for things to be fixed, remember it has to be broken before a fix can be applied. When you pray for strength, God will reveal your weaknesses, so you know what to work on.

When we work on strengthening our muscles, the body becomes sore and achy. This alone motivates you to work harder so that the soreness goes away. It is the same way with our prayers to God he will answer but please understand what you are asking for. Let me pause to encourage you for this moment, that trouble don't last always. As I kept reading this prayer over and over, I realized how much of it had been manifested in my life. Communication with God regularly will always keep you motivated. His word says I can do all things through Christ who strengtheneth me. (Philippians 4:13) KJV. Notice I did not say it would be an easy journey but with God on your side it will be a successful. The reward is knowing you have pleased God in your coming in and going out of the assignments we have been given.

The most important and most difficult assignment for remaining on the journey was M-E. Just me. Not my enemy, but my INNER ME! I had lots of excuses and constant indecisiveness . I was so busy telling God what I could not do because I felt so inadequate at the time that I didn't hear HIM say that this is what will be so. So, my motivation came as I was developing my relationship with God. However, I didn't think I would make a difference, but I know I wanted to. God is a patient God. And He's faithful and just. He gives us one chance after another chance after another chance. As a songwriter once wrote, *I'm glad I serve a God of another chance because I messed up my second chance a long time ago.*

Because I asked God a long time ago to forgive me for grieving him and for having no trust, he empowered me to continue moving forward in this journey with Him. Like the soldier, you must stay on the battlefield for the Lord because God said to me, My grace is sufficient for thee: for my strength is made perfect in weakness. Most gladly therefore will I rather glory in my infirmities, that the power of Christ may rest upon me. 10 Therefore I take pleasure in infirmities, in reproaches, in necessities, in persecutions, in distresses for Christ's sake: for when I am weak, then am I strong. (2 Corinthians 9-10) KJV.

I had to trust God because no one else would do. Not even my closest friends, or my family could stand with me on the journey I accepted, and that God ordained in my life. Even still to this day, I function one day at a time. First, we are not guaranteed any time. We all have the same amount of time in each day. It is what we do with it that makes the difference. The devil likes for us to be busy so we can't hear or focus on God and then we allow our loose lips to speak negative things into the atmosphere and our idle minds to wander into dark and dirty places. I know what I am talking about because I have been there. The bible tells us that we live by every word that proceeds out of our mouth. To survive on the journey, you must speak life, speak holiness, and speak prosperity. Tell God thank you for things that you don't even see yet. He said that we could call it into existence as though it is already done. God said it, not Kathy! It is no secret that I am a lover of gospel music. So, I have to share the words of the songwriter lyrics that say, *sometimes you have to encourage yourself; sometimes you have to speak victory during your test. No matter how you feel speak the word and you will be healed, speak over yourself, encourage yourself in the Lord.*

The real truth to everything that we do is that we are nothing without God. Everything that we say or do should be for HIS glory. We can't take credit for anything. Even as I sit here and write these words, I already know that none of this is about me or any accomplishments that make me think for a moment that I did something great. Let's keep it real, I'm not as patient as God requires me to be but God is patient and I strive to be like HIM. We can't duplicate the patience of God, but he wants us to try to look like him every day. God is Faithful. To be faithful, we have to be like God because any other effort is useless and unsuccessful. He asks us for just a mustard seed size of faith. My testimony helped me to increase my faith, I can honestly say there are still times I have to work on trusting God for everything that I need in me and my family's lives. I'm trying to keep this as real as possible. I know it sounds like hype, but I can testify that a check showed up in my mailbox on more than one occasion, when the money was low, and we didn't know if the bills would get paid or we could not by food to eat-although we did not lose any weight because of it. God is a healer. I can testify that my family member was on his deathbed and his healing and restoration confuse the doctors, the staff, and the hospital. Yes, I trust HIM. Trusting him is something you do. Yes, I trust HIM. Life and living motivated me to trust God. Now I understand why the old folks use to say, "just keep living, baby!". I encourage you to allow the love that God has for each of us to lead you to a place of courage, thankfulness, and obedience. Let your YES in God be YES. Do it every day!

What scriptures, books or resources do you recommend using when you are looking to grow in your walk with God?

After I had messed up again while allowing God to be Lord of my life, here I was getting *another* chance. I lived in Anchorage Alaska for four years, October 1986 until December 1990. I did not have a desire to even go there because I did not have a clue as to how all of this would work out for my good. I had a very rebellious attitude, and I kept waiting for the opportunity to say, "I knew this would not work out". But after experiencing more turmoil in my marriage that I could hardly bare, loss of so many loved ones and what felt like a tsunami of grief and heartache of my daily living, God was the only safe haven and comforting place I could go. So, I sought and poured myself into developing a relationship with God, It took me looking at those mountains in Alaska that encircled me, the peace of a winter's night snowfall and the freedom and liberty of the Alaskan wildlife to see GOD as AWESOME and MAJESTIC! That's why I was there.

One very cold night I was standing outside my car on my way inside the house and I looked up into the sky and saw what was called the northern lights. The Northern lights would always take on an image of a majestic being. This night the image appeared as a Majestic God flowing in the ice crystals in the sky with his outstretched arms towards me to let me know He loved me and was there waiting for me to accept His love, His grace and His mercy. I heard Him say enter this relationship with me and receive Me unto yourself. As the tears flowed from my eyes which God would not allow to freeze on my face, I knew this was real and I was ready to learn and move towards being the "best me" that God would be proud to call me his daughter.

When I began my transformation, I went to bible studies and women fellowships and attending retreats trying to stay focused on what was in front of me while still battling the things of the world that were all around me. One particular retreat was in the Alaska cabins in the mountains that appeared very isolated, I confessed my life before a congregation of women I barely knew. My burden lifted, and the chains were broken, and I was set free to explore my journey. HALLELUJAH! PRAISE GOD!

When you are looking to grow in your walk with God, just tell God what you want. The bible says, *"Trust in the Lord, and do good; Dwell in the land, and feed on His faithfulness. Delight yourself also in the Lord, And He shall give you the desires of your heart"*. (Psalms 37:3-4) NKJV .

I know I've made it sound easy, but it is up to you how your journey will play out. Your first reference for growth is your bible. Bibles come in many versions and some of them can affect your understanding. I selected the King James Version as my source when I was trying to increase my relationship with God. I set in my basement in Anchorage, Alaska and attempted to read the word so I could get an understanding of how to live for Christ. Wow! The KJV was like reading Greek. So, I said to God, I do not understand what this is saying. God responded and told me to turn off my television. So, I turned the down the volume and read again. But still my understanding was foreign. God repeated himself and said turn the television off. Being the mouthy, "I'm in control person that I was back then" I said, "I turned it down, so the television is not bothering me or affecting my understanding". He said again to turn the television off. This time I did it and return to reading from the King James Version. As I did, the words popped of the page for me and my understanding was made clear. God wasn't trying to suggest a version of the bible for me to read, He was letting me know that as I draw close to him, he would draw close to me. I wanted so much to get to know God for myself. I still have moments with the King James Version so you may want to try other versions that are translated for your understanding.

I have always been drawn to books that are regarding my purpose, the power in the blood of Jesus, and the anointing of the Holy Spirit. I mentioned two books that I have read that speaks to my walk with God, "The Blood (also, Good Morning Holy Spirt)" by Benny Hinn and The Purpose Driven Life by Rick Warren. These are great books for me, and I was at a place in my life that I needed to be excited about the God that I served and get a better understanding of where I was headed. I recommend these books to anyone seeking to get a closer walk - a closer relationship with God. One of the many scriptures that I love, reads:

1I will bless the Lord at all times: his praise shall continually be in my mouth.

2My soul shall make her boast in the Lord: the humble shall hear thereof and be glad.

3O magnify the Lord with me and let us exalt his name together.

4I sought the Lord, and he heard me, and delivered me from all my fears. (Psalms 34:1-4)

Read Psalms 34 it in its entirety. Let it bless your life. God bless you on your journey.

Kathy Daniel

Kathy L. Daniel, a woman of many gifts and talents, began her life in the pursuit of happiness like any other young woman desiring to have a family and career. Shortly after completing one year of college, she married her high school sweetheart in 1980. Her marriage to First Sergeant Autry B. Daniel, Jr., Msgt, United States Air Force was blessed with two children, a smart and beautiful daughter, Angela Dionne and a brilliant son Anthony Bryan. They raised their children while serving our country for 20 years and then moved to Texas to set up permanent residence.

In pursuit of her education, Kathy received an Associate Degree in Accounting (AS) from Western Oklahoma State College, Altus Oklahoma, a Bachelor Degree in Marketing (BS) from the University of Alaska Anchorage, then later earned an MBA from The Keller Graduate School of Business.

After working years in the Banking / Financial Industry, God shifted Kathy's goal from Corporate America to establishing her as an Entrepreneur, which birthed her business, Inspired By God (IBG) Graphic Designs. IBG's target audience consisted of non-profit organizations, churches and individuals. This designation allowed more opportunity for ministry exposure and Kathy was able to touch and affect the lives of many. She is also a lover of gospel music. She participates with her own church choir, Rhema Life Church Plano, The Dallas Chapter of the Gospel Music Workshop of America, and The Texas Mass Choir, all of which she holds leadership positions.

Kathy is an ambitious Woman of God with a sweet spirit. She is compassionate and giving, supportive and trust-worthy, fun-loving and caring. Kathy is a hard worker with a great sense for planning and implementing. She will get the job done.

Barbara Hollace
Yes, God!

Each of us has a journey that God has taken us on. There are moments that occur along that journey that really help to shape and define who we are. Share one of those Yes, God moments you have encountered, where you had to trust Him without knowing all the steps.

"With man this is impossible, but with God all things are possible." (Matthew 19:26)

From the moment I heard his labored breathing and saw his mottled skin, I knew we were in trouble. My husband was gasping for breath. It was time for action.

"We need to call 911 now!" I said firmly.

"We can wait awhile," my husband said, between gasps.

"No, we can't. I'm calling them now." Help was only a few blocks away.

After I disconnected the call, I laid my hands on my husband and prayed that God would restore the breath of life. I rebuked the enemy and covered Bill with the blood of the Lamb through prayer. And I began what would be the prayer I breathed with my every breath for weeks to come, "No weapon formed against you will prosper."

After a quick examination by the medics and a fruitless breathing treatment, the hospital was our next stop. But even as I watched my husband walk down the eight steps from our apartment to the waiting gurney, I knew the Lord's strength would go with him in this battle. With his eyes, Bill conveyed the message asking for my help and my presence to go with him.

"I'll be right there. I'll drive the car to meet you."

Throwing necessities into a backpack, I grabbed my purse and continued to pray. I didn't know what was happening, but God did. My only hope was to trust Him.

When I arrived at the hospital and entered the Emergency Room, I found Bill in a cubicle with nurses attending to him. We soon discovered that his heart was in AFib, and after a series of tests, determined that he also had pneumonia. How Bill bypassed the flu and ended up with pneumonia we didn't understand, all we knew was that he was a sick man.

To make matters worse, a flu epidemic had hit the area in early January and ICU beds were at a premium. Literally across the state, there were no ICU beds. At one point we were told, Bill might need to be transferred to Missoula, Montana or Seattle, Washington. We live in Spokane, Washington. Either place would be hours away. This couldn't be happening. Crying out to God, in my heart, I pleaded, "Lord, make a way, where there seems to be no way."

After eight hours in the ER, they finally found a bed for Bill in ICU. We got settled in for the journey even though we didn't know the destination. Part of my brain believed it would be a simple fix, and my heart knew that it likely was not. Bill was concerned about me; I was more concerned about him. I was confident that God was bigger than all of it.

But it got worse. I had taken up residence in Bill's room for the night. I would not leave him with things so uncertain. About midnight the doctor came in and woke us up asking if Bill was having any chest pains. Bill said, "No." The doctor said, "We think you're having a heart attack because your heart enzyme count is so elevated compared to when you came in. We may have to send you to another hospital in the morning to have a heart cath procedure done."

I heard the words, but I couldn't believe it. It seemed like an episode from a television show, not our lives. All I knew to do was pray. I rallied prayer warriors across the United States and the world to pray with me through the night. The next blood draw at 4 a.m. would determine the course of treatment. Truly we needed a miracle!

In the middle of the night, God and I had a conversation. Through my tears, I had to choose which path I would take, the path of faith or the path of fear. I chose the path of faith. I prayed on the full armor of God from Ephesians 6 and by the authority of Jesus, I entered into deep intercessory prayer as I pleaded for Bill's life and that God would change the enzyme level in his blood. In those hours between midnight and 4 a.m., I prayed like I have never prayed before. I prayed believing that we would see the manifestation of the miracle God had for us. And while others joined with me, I knew that God would hear our prayers.

As a seasoned prayer warrior, I approached the throne room of grace and point-blank asked God if Bill would live or if he would be taken from me. My first husband had died from cancer 25 years earlier, but this time, I knew the fight was different. God told me that Bill would live. I was fighting from a place of victory, but the battle would be intense. There would be healing for both Bill and for me. It was time for old scars to be healed as God took me to a new level.

Bill's blood was drawn right on schedule and then we waited for the morning rounds. When the doctor arrived, she had good news. Bill's enzyme level had dropped by 50% in four hours, so the test was not needed. Thank you, Lord!

But the battle had just begun. There is too much of the story to cover here. The highlights include that in the first five days of his hospitalization he had pneumonia, a heart attack, contracted Influenza A, and the next morning had a brain bleed (stroke) which resulted in brain surgery to remove the pool of blood in his brain.

Any of those things could have killed a man, but God had determined that my husband, a 74-year-old man, who had smoked for years, would be the stage on which God performed a miracle, not just one, but many miracles. Bill was away from home 168 days, most of those in ICU units, in five hospitals and a skilled nursing facility (for a short time) in two different states, followed by continued home care, with me as the primary caregiver.

Time and time again, God brought us to the cross where Jesus died so we might live. I learned the magnitude of the resurrection power of Jesus as I watched my husband come to death's door again and again, and God say, "No, it's not his time."

From the moment I left our home at 5 a.m. on the morning of January 10, 2018, I began a walk of faith where God led us into unknown territory. I thank God that I didn't know what was ahead of us because I'm not sure I could have withstood the ocean wave of emotions that would have consumed me.

But instead the moment I said, "Yes, God, I surrender my will to You, and I will follow where You lead", God took me by the hand and led me over mountains and through deep valleys. There were raging rivers that He parted so we could walk through on dry ground. We went through the desert places when my husband was sedated and couldn't communicate. All I could do was cry out to God and pray over Bill and speak words of life and sing praises to the Lord for the miracles that were coming.

God transformed me. God stripped away the extraneous things in my life and there were only two priorities: God and Bill. That is where my focus remained. However, there was something more that God asked of me. Instead of walking through this deep valley privately, God asked me to invite others in to see His handiwork. Not only those on my prayer warriors email list, but God asked me to take our journey to Facebook, because He "wanted to do a work there."

For most of our lives we have kept our personal life private. The door is only open to a few chosen friends. God wanted that door to be opened to the world, the world of Facebook, of all places.

I said, "Yes, God" because I knew that His plan and purpose was greater than what I could see. I believe that either you trust God, or you don't, there is no in-between place or space. I trusted God and I still do today.

On the dark days when even the doctors were discouraged, God showed me a little sign of life. I had hope and sometimes it was my hope that ignited the hope of the medical staff that tended to Bill. God showed me life and I would fight for my husband's life, no matter what it took. When you have the power of God behind you, and the fire of God burning in your heart, you can take on any Goliath in your life.

Those who followed our journey were asked to pray for Bill's needs. God loves specific prayers because it gives Him an opportunity to show what He can do. I believe it gives us the same opportunity that Jesus gave the blind man, "What do you want me to do for you?" He wants us to admit our need so He can help us.

God was my strength every day. I had to ask others to help me when I was overwhelmed by the magnitude of what was happening. For example, I was too distracted to drive. I knew it and a dear friend offered to take me to the hospital in the morning and pick me up at night. God provided for us in so many ways.

And the miracles kept happening one step at a time. Some of the decisions I had to make about Bill's care caused me to face my fears and trust God with my husband's life and that He was writing a new script for my life, too. Often the past has a hold on us, sometimes without our knowledge. God wanted not only to save one life, He wanted to save both of us and equip us for the next chapter of our lives.

Even today, I continue to say Yes God I choose to follow you as we continue on Bill's road to recovery. He has improved so much, but God is not finished yet. Hallelujah!

How has this journey changed me? First, I have become a fiercer prayer warrior. I will pray anytime, anywhere for those who need prayer. It is time each of us use the fire God has placed in our hearts to light the fire of hope in others. Two, I am not defined by my fears. I choose faith. I trust God to meet my needs and when faced with an unknown situation, I run to God first. Ask for wisdom and then walk in the way He commands. Three, our lives have been forever changed. The life we had will never be again. But that's not a bad thing. When God has a path, a passion, and a purpose for you, pruning will be required. It is a promise for those who love Him that He will equip them. "The reality is that the Lord never calls the qualified; He qualifies the called." — Henry Blackaby

And lastly, where God leads, He provides. Help and provision will come from unexpected places and people. *"Where does my help come from? My help comes from the Lord, Maker of heaven and earth."* (Psalm 121:1-2)

When God presents you with an impossible situation, remember the verse from Matthew 19:26, *"With man this is impossible, but with God all things are possible."* Then step out in faith, clothed in the full armor of God. Pray without ceasing and trust God without reservation. He is faithful and He will do it.

How did you develop your faith when it seemed like nothing was going right in your life? Share a situation where you had to develop your faith walk.

When God says, "It's time" you obey, no matter the consequences. In 2007 my husband and I were on-site managers at a low-income apartment building. When you live in the heart of the city, there is action day and night. We knew that God had called us to serve in this place no matter how difficult it was. Year after year, we heard the question, "When are you leaving?" Our reply, "When God says it's time."

There was a lot of stress that came with the job and my husband's blood pressure was rising. His doctor suggested he find another occupation or retire. When we realized that staying there could cost my husband his life, we knew that God was sending us a warning. It was time to go.

On Valentine's Day 2007, we gave each other the gift of life as we turned in our letters of resignation and gave our two weeks' notice. There was a catch. It was one reason we had been cautious about making this move. It wasn't just our job/income that we were walking away from, it was also our home. Writing that letter meant we would trust God for the next step, because we didn't have one.

How could we find a job when Bill's health was in question? Our faith in God was being tested. Either God would catch us or teach us to fly. As we neared our departure date, there wasn't a door that mysteriously opened. It was ironic. As property managers we had served not only the low-income population, but also the homeless. Now we found ourselves soon to be homeless. We were in good company. Many of the men and women in the bible that God used didn't have a place of their own to lay their head, from Abraham to Jesus and many more in between.

Our good friends said we could come and stay in their basement for a little while. Nothing seemed to be happening on the time schedule we envisioned. Our stay turned into three months.

And then we found a three-month dog sitting gig for two basset hounds. Sound like an adventure? Oh yes, it was! Again, so many things went wrong! It was one of the hottest summers on record with temps over 100 degrees. One month the owner of the dogs didn't pay the power bill and the power was turned off on one of those 100 + degree days. I was working for a friend and my husband called me and told me what happened. "What?!?!!?" After a few phone calls and lots of prayer, miraculously the power company came back the same day and turned it back on. Only the hand of God could have pulled off that miracle.

It went from bad to worse. The dogs were used to sleeping in the bedroom with their owner, and with us, the dogs were in their kennels in the other bedroom. They were not happy, so they howled -loudly. So, we invited them into the bedroom where we were sleeping on an air mattress. Their nails were sharp, and they punctured the air mattress, on more than one occasion. My husband wasn't very excited about waking up flat on the floor.

And last, but not least, I sprained my ankle while I was out walking the dogs. Going up three flights of stairs on a sprained ankle was difficult. Bill was stuck with dog duty alone, day and night. It felt like were living a modern-day Job story. I continued to pray and believe that God would open a door. We had heard His voice and were walking in obedience to the best of our ability. Yet the refining fire kept purifying us.

We still had not found a replacement income for what we had lost. I prayed, "Lord, show us the way." All the doors seemed closed and we were free falling. My husband could retire but I had a long way to go until retirement age.

"Lord, what can I do?"
The Lord replied, "What is the passion of your heart?"

My response, "Writing is the passion of my heart."
"Then go do it," He replied.

I was a law school graduate and had a business degree, surely, I could find something. My first thought was the career placement office of my old alma mater at Gonzaga Law School. After explaining my predicament, Emily was very helpful in helping me track down options for a telecommuting job. With my husband's health issues, it seemed like an ideal situation to work from home.

Soon things fell in place. Bill's retirement funding came through. I found a telecommuting job that fit my credentials and we found a new place to live outside of the city. A place where birds were singing, there were trees and open spaces, no more concrete jungle, we were so grateful! And God led us to the "right church" only a couple of blocks from our home.

What was the secret to growing our faith during that time period? Never giving up on God. Staying faithful in prayer and trusting God was working all things together for our good even when our eyes couldn't see the outcome.

Another valuable lesson we learned was not to compromise our integrity or our standards. God calls us to be pure and holy, not just when things are going well, but even through life's challenges. We held on to God's hand and we held on to each other. The best thing to remember when you walk through life's challenges with your spouse is that the battle is against things in the world, not fighting against each other. You are on the same team! Keep your eyes on the Lord even when you don't understand, and He will carry you through.

How did you stay motivated in seasons where patience, faith and trust had to be exercised?

Over the years, I have learned that to survive and thrive not only in my Christian walk, but in every facet of life, I must be intimately connected to God. "I am the vine; you are the branches. If you remain in me and I in you, you will bear much fruit; apart from me you can do nothing." (John 15:5) This verse sums up not only our goal as Christians but the secret to success in life.

Like many other Christian leaders, I discovered that 4 a.m. was the best time to meet with God. Not only to dive into the Bible, but to listen to His voice and talk with Him about life. In those early morning hours when most of the neighborhood, and much of the world, is still sleeping, the noise is at a minimum, and tranquility and peace are my companions. It is in the noise and chaos of life that we lose our way.

How do we build trust in our relationships? By spending time with another person. And it is in communication with God that our trust grows so that in the storm's roar or the silence of the night or the chaos of a hospital, we know God is with us even when earthly circumstances may lead us to a different conclusion.

I have learned the discipline of spending time with God daily and then praying without ceasing during the day. How is motivation tied to the discipline of a quiet time? Because of the result. Amazing peace, joy, wisdom and victory are the outcome of time spent in His presence. It has become a way of life for me. It's not something that I "have" to do - it's something I want to do.

As soon as I get up in the morning, I go to my office and open the Bible and companion devotional. It is a quiet place. It is a holy place where I invite God to spend time with me. I long for our time together like a thirsty man desires water.

Seasons of prayer and fasting bring me to a deeper place with God. If there is a specific person that needs prayer or an event that I am planning, I will organize a day of prayer and fasting and invite others to join me. Our church has made a practice of setting aside October as a month of prayer and fasting, to prepare for the November elections. What a great opportunity to come together with other believers and multiply the impact of our prayers. "Where two or three are gathered together in my name, there I am in the midst of them." (Matthew 18:20)

During my husband's health challenges in 2018, I came to realize that the years of spending time alone with God, no matter how busy my schedule, had prepared me for this season of my life. My husband and I learned about emergency preparedness during the years we managed a low-income apartment building and homeless shelter. It is so important to be prepared so you can successfully navigate a disaster, but even more so, when you are a leader and others are looking to you for answers in a crisis.

It wasn't until months into my husband's health crisis that I realized that emergency preparedness is not only a necessity in the physical realm but also the spiritual realm. When you are in the middle of crisis, yes, God will hear your cries for help, as you feel you are drowning. How much better to intimately know the captain of your ship on the calm seas before the tsunami waves threaten to capsize your lifeboat?

For years in those early morning hours as I sought God's face, in praise and worship, through the good times and the bad, through both my laughter and my tears, God was shaping me and pruning me to be of service to Him. What a privilege and honor to shine brightly for the Lord when you are going through your own dark night because you know that He can be trusted with your present and your future.

It may seem that the result, your goal, is long in coming but I am reminded of the verse from Ecclesiastes 3:11, "He has made everything beautiful in its time." The question is: Am I willing to trust God with the outcome? Do I trust Him to do what's best for me or my loved one? I believe that often we grow impatient and, in the process, we will settle for "good enough" or maybe "better." But it is the true warrior of the faith who is willing to hold on through the twists and turns of life as they claim the reward of "God's best" for them.

When life knocks me down, all I can do is look up. My ego lays slain on the altar, my goals and dreams tossed aside like leaves in the wind, and there with my soul laid bare before the Lord, I confess my faith in Him who is the giver of life. "Now faith is the substance of things hoped for, the evidence of things not seen." (Hebrews 11:1) It's never too late to get started on building your relationship with your heavenly Father. Start today. There is a great cloud of witnesses that is cheering you on.

What scriptures, books or resources do you recommend using when you are looking to grow in your walk with God?

Scriptures:

Ephesians 6:10-18 (The full armor of God) It must be in place as we fight our battles.

Isaiah 54:17: *"No weapon formed against you shall prosper, and every tongue which rises against you in judgment You shall condemn. This is the heritage of the servants of the LORD, and their righteousness is from Me,"* says the LORD.

Isaiah 43:1-2: *"But now, this is what the LORD says—he who created you, Jacob, he who formed you, Israel: "Do not fear, for I have redeemed you; I have summoned you by name; you are mine. When you pass through the waters, I will be with you; and when you pass through the rivers, they will not sweep over you. When you walk through the fire, you will not be burned; the flames will not set you ablaze."*

Psalm 23: The Lord is my shepherd, I shall lack nothing…

Jeremiah 29:11: *"For I know the plans I have for you,"* declares the LORD, *"plans to prosper you and not to harm you, plans to give you hope and a future."*

Philippians 4:13: *"I can do all things through Christ who strengthens me".*

Nehemiah 8:10: Do not grieve, for the joy of the Lord is your strength.

Matthew 19:26: Jesus looked at them and said, "With man this is impossible, but with God all things are possible."

Isaiah 40:31 They that wait upon the Lord shall renew their strength, they will mount up on wings like eagles, they will run and not be weary, they will walk and not be faint.

Books:

- *Draw the Circle: The 40-day Prayer Challenge* by Mark Batterson

- *The Circle Maker: Praying Circles Around Your Greatest Dreams and Biggest Fears* by Mark Batterson
- *Girls with Swords: How to Carry Your Cross Like a Hero* by Lisa Bevere
- *My Utmost for His Highest* by Oswald Chambers
- *In His Steps* by Charles Sheldon

Resources:
- Prayer team to encircle you – both in person and via other mediums including social media, text, email, phone calls.
- Cultivate friendships and accountability partners.
- Mentors: Personally, and professionally (Iron sharpens iron.)

Hymns:

The old hymns of the faith are filled with good doctrine and encouragement about how to draw closer to God. Buy a hymnal that you can hold in your hands. Sing out loud and make a joyful noise to the Lord. It empowers you and makes the devil flee.

My favorite hymns:

It is Well with My Soul
O For a Thousand Tongues to Sing
Abide with Me
Amazing Grace

The Old Rugged Cross
Turn Your Eyes Upon Jesus
In the Garden
Mine Eyes Have Seen the Glory
God Will Take Care of You
Faith is the Victory

Barbara Hollace

Barbara Hollace is a Christian woman who loves the Lord. God has called her to be a prayer warrior and a writer. Her greatest joy is to pray for others and see God's miracles happen. Through her own husband's health challenges, Barbara has learned that prayer can move mountains in our lives.

Her love of writing blossomed from an early age when she created her own greeting cards for family and friends. In 1985, Barbara self-published her first poetry book, "From Dust to Dust." Since that time Barbara has been published in 18 books and numerous newspaper articles. She has written 13 novels and is pursuing publication options.

Professionally, she is an author, editor, writing coach, and speaker. Owner of Hollace Writing Services, Barbara's goal is to "identify the good and magnify it!" This includes helping a person get the story in their heart on the page, editing the story, and pursuing publication options. She recently opened her own publishing company, Hollace House Publishing, and will expand its reach in the upcoming years.

Barbara has a Bachelor's degree in Business Administration from Western Washington University and a

Juris Doctor degree from Gonzaga University School of Law. She is also the Communications Director for Spokane Dream Center church in Spokane Valley, Washington.

Barbara and her husband live in Eastern Washington and love to vacation at the ocean. For more information about Barbara and her business, go to www.barbarahollace.com.

Pearl Chiarenza
Yes, God!

Each of us has a journey that God has taken us on. There are moments that occur along that journey that really helped to shape and define who we are. Share one of those Yes, God moments you have encountered, where you had to trust Him without knowing all the steps.

One of my most remembrable God moments was when we were trying to have our second child. It was two years after adopting our first child after 10 years of infertility and we were trying another infertility procedure. After about three months into the process they found that I had a fibroid tumor on my ovaries, and we would need to stop to deal with the fibroid. Of course, I was frustrated and was thinking and wondering why after spending thousands of dollars to get this far why was this happening. I had to trust in God that he had it under control while being upset, we were being delayed again. Were we meant to not have another child?

Fast forward about eight months later we are in the next process of infertility treatment. I have just completed the egg retrieval and the doctor said they only retrieved three eggs. We left hoping for the best and left it in God's hands.

Well, twenty-four hours later they call and ask us to come in. So, as we are driving to the doctor our thoughts are well it didn't work so they are bringing us in to let us know. Boy did God show up big time. After, fifteen years of either fibroid tumor surgeries and infertility treatments he gave up a HUGE blessing. The doctors were letting us know that while they were working and trying to get the procedure of egg fertilization to happen naturally it was not happening. They did the ICSI treatment which would be an addition

$10,000! Well Chuck and I looked at each other and knew there was no way we could afford it as our insurance would not cover it. As we shared that with the doctors, they looked at us and said there was nothing to worry about. They believe in what they do, and they would not charge us for it. had to agree to follow the doctor's orders precisely. Well right than did I know that could only be a God moment and that our little family of three would grow to four because of his grace over the doctors and us!

How did you develop your faith when it seemed like nothing was going right in your life? Share a situation where you had to develop your faith walk.

We had just moved to Florida and shortly after arriving my Dad decided he wanted a divorce, and, he was trying to transfer all assets without my mother finding out. We helped my mom with an attorney. One task given was to inventory items in the home. In doing so my mom realized some of her heirlooms were missing. As mom and I are discussing the items my oldest who was seven at the time became agitated. Finally, he said please stop worrying about them it is ok. When I inquired further why he was so upset he let me know that his Papa (my Dad) had threatened him that if he told that Papa sold those items without Grandma knowing he would never be able to see him or Grandma again. I became so upset. My children were unhappy with our move to Florida and my job was not going as well as planned. I was so frustrated as I thought everything was planned out. My parents would come to Florida in the winter months enabling my boys to be closer to their grandparents and I could work from home enabling me to be there when they came home from school. All this was turned upside down. As this was happening, I had plans and attended a women's retreat at church. One evening we sat with our priest for him to receive our prayers. As I shared what was happening with my parents and the actions of my dad, he shared a statement I have carried the rest of my life forward. Father Bill said "You do not get to pick your parents that is God's plan. However, God helps you with making the rules in your ballgame of life so while you will always love them if they need to sit on the bench while the you are calling plays of success than that is where they need to sit. Once they can accept your rules of the game you can let them back in." WOW POWERFUL WORDS!

Well my ballgame never saw my mom sit out because she respected my wishes. However, my Dad had to sit out for about five years. When I let him back into the game, he played well enough to move in with us. While living with us he broke rules again by becoming racial towards my oldest son. As I found out the terrible things, he did I realize with pray and God's guidance that my Dad would have to take a permanent seat on the bench. It was a hard decision and I know God lead me to the decision with strong conviction.

How did you stay motivated in season where patience, faith and trust had to be exercised?

The situation with my dad was very hard as I was a Daddy's girl. As we went thru the challenges with my Dad, I knew I need to trust God's plan for him and me, to trust that only he knew the plan and to keep praying for guidance. As I prayed God revealed additional horrible things that my dad did to my son. I prayed to God to show me how to release myself from my Dad so that I could move forward without feeling bad about it. It was a biggie he showed me. God revealed I needed to write an obituary to my Dad and the things he had done. I trusted God to help me write it and as I wrote this it enabled me to release all feelings of anger, hate and disappointment.

What scriptures, books or resources do you recommend using when you are looking to grow in your walk with God?

I love Joyce Meyers books, I have a friend who has a closed group offering prayer and scriptures I listen to every day and recently started reading the bible again with a new bible group to keep my mind focused on his message.

Pearl Chiarenza

As the owner of Bodyworks Health & Wellness Center for the past six years Pearl has seen her clients collectively lose over 8,000 pounds. She has personally lost 57 pounds and has maintained her weight loss over the past eight years. Pearl understands that to give fully to others, we must first take care of ourselves. It is one of the reasons she founded Bodyworks Health & Wellness Center in 2011. Pearl's remarkable passion for sharing her knowledge (and weight loss journey) has been a major contributing factor to Bodyworks continued visibility and success.

She also lends her time to coordinating multiple events through a network called Women's Successful Living, that assists women who have faced economic and personal challenges. Working one-on-one with individuals Pearl encourages them to set goals and journal about their struggles and successes along with emphasizing the importance to schedule time for self-care and physical activity.

Pearl has been married to her husband Charles for 29 years and is mom to son Matthew. She balances her commitment to her family, her business, and her community involvement, which includes Rotary International, Brandon Service League and the Sylvia Thomas Center, with much grace and finesse.

Her dedication in giving to others is seemingly endless as she regularly holds sponsorship contests for those who cannot afford Bodyworks weight loss programs, as well she partners with a domestic violence non-profit to mentor children in need.

Bodyworks has been voted "Best of Brandon" and "Best of Southshore" Weight Loss Clinic in the Tampa metro area (what years?). Our clients are local residents as well as leaders and executives of well-known corporations.

Liz Brewer
Yes, God!

"If you've knelt beside the rubble of an aching broken heart, when the things you gave your life to fell apart, you're not the first to be acquainted with sorrow, grief or pain. But the master promised sunshine after rain". These are the words of the song penned by Bill Gaither in Joy Comes in the Morning.

Those words sound good when pieced together but when life seems to be a series of tragedies, one by one, one may truly wonder why? Why does this keep happening? What did I do to deserve this? So many thoughts fill your mind and you just want to escape. But it is in the very deepest, darkest night that I tell you, you will feel the loving arms of our savior, Jesus.

I remember it clearly, as I was singing in the service one Sunday in early 2017, I could hear a voice so clearly tell me, "I am the answer", As I looked around the stage to see if anyone else could hear it, I realized I must have been hearing things. But I heard it again in the second service, then once again in the next. I knew at that moment God was speaking to me. As I struggled to understand what he meant, I then also heard His words in my spirit telling me that I needed to write a book and that would be the title. Of course, time went on and life was filled with a lot of busy things, work, family, graduations and, sadly, deaths. But it was apparent to me that this was not just something I heard in my head but was an "assignment" that God has given me. But how does one write and publish a book? I had no idea where to start.

Fast forward to January 2019, while leading one of my Connections events, that a friend asked me if I would be interested in being a part of a book called, Yes, God. Yes, the book you now hold in your hand. While this isn't the "book" that He assigned me to write, this is a short version of what God has laid on my heart. According to experts, an unexpected death of a loved one is the most reported traumatic experience one can deal with in their lifetime and, , can cause psychiatric disorders.

Over the past several years, my life has consisted of one death after another of people who were close to me. Death seems to follow me, yet, I believe it is through these losses I have gained life. Part of the cycle of life is, living and dying. We all should be prepared for it and in most cases, when we age, we have a peace upon one's passing because we know they have lived a full life. But what I learned is that when death comes unexpectedly, it can shake your entire world and make you question everything you have ever believed in. It fills you with incredible grief that hurts to the core. A pain that you cannot describe in words. A loss that feels like you cannot breathe. It makes you question, is God there and if He is, then why would He take them so soon?

I believe my faith journey began in my mid 20's when, during a women's bible study, I realized that I didn't have a testimony to share like all the other "older" women did. When I would listen to the other ladies talk about their struggles and share their praise reports, for some odd reason, I felt left out. I know that sounds crazy because who wants to have struggles and crosses to bear?

Nothing traumatic had ever happened to me and my husband and I were living a normal life raising our son. My husband, Jeff, was working at the local power plant and while his long work hours and varied shifts meant my son and I had a lot of time alone, we were happy. We were building a life together and life was good. I was active in my church singing and leading Bible studies and my faith was growing.

My daily prayers consisted of thanking God for my blessings and for the life He gave me. I remember telling God that I didn't have a testimony and that I while I was thankful for my blessings, I felt like I should have a testimony to share. They say be careful what you pray for. All that would change the day I received a call that my husband was in an accident at work. I remember going into my assistant's office after I received the call and telling her that I needed to leave to go to the hospital because my husband, Jeff, was being medevaced to the hospital. She grabbed her purse and told me I wouldn't be driving as this didn't sound good. Jeff had been in a crane accident and his leg had been broken in multiple places. While they tried to save his leg by placing pins in it, after 48 hours his vital organs shut down and they told us he may not survive if we didn't take drastic measures. The doctors shared with us that the only option to save his life was to amputate his leg. As a young wife, the decision fell upon me to make the decision that would forever change my husband of 27 years old's life. It was my responsibility to make the decision that he would have to live with for the rest of his life. I would do anything to not risk losing the love of my life and I would be there for him no matter what but the weight of the decision I needed to make was incredibly heavy. The days that followed were filled with great sadness and as I saw him dealing with the effects of losing a limb, what surprised me, and everyone around us, was the incredible strength and courage he showed despite this new normal he would have to accept. Although we knew he was in incredible pain, he continued to make us laugh. During services one Sunday, several months after his accident, our Pastor asked Jeff to share his experience with the church. It was there he told them that while he was lying on his back in the helicopter on the way to the hospital, he told God that if he would give him one more chance, he would rededicate his life to him. As I stood there with tears rolling down my cheeks, not out of sadness, but of joy, I remembered the conversation I had with God years earlier and realized that even though this is not what I could have ever wanted, I believe God now I had a testimony.

Jeff's outlook on life had changed. When looking at death square in the face, you realize how precious life is. When you are so close to death and your life is hanging by a thread, it makes you realize that no amount of work, accolades or big paychecks can ever give you the joy you have, but don't appreciate.

For several years, I shared my faith journey of his accident and the various struggles we faced and how our faith has carried us through. I spoke at our Women's Retreat about how important it is for us to recognize that God can turn tragedy into good, if we recognize it. After several years of dealing with his accident, the financial stresses a toll. Our income was cut in half as my husband faced years of physical therapy and learning how to walk again. But God was there in the midst of it all. When we would worry about the constant bill collectors calling and threatening us and not know how we would pay the mortgage, God showed up. After coming so close to losing my husband, every day we had together was a gift because we had each other. You start to realize that this is the small stuff in the big scheme. We would carry on. We recognized God was in control of every aspect of our life and we trusted Him daily. After many prayer-filled nights, and three long years of legal battles, we moved into a new chapter in our life. We had our second child and my husband returned to college to complete his degree.

Our faith grew solid and I saw God in a different light. God became our Provider. It was new to me to be able to have that faith knowledge that He would provide and meet all of our needs, just as he promised. We opened a business for my husband and built a new home. The joy of knowing we were together filled all our days. The joy that filled my soul was one that no one could ever take away.

Several years passed and we received the news we were pregnant with our third child. We were elated! But our elation soon turned to sadness. At 7 weeks of excitement of our coming baby, we experienced a miscarriage. Our doctor told us it was not unusual to lose a baby that early and that we could try again. We had experienced a miscarriage before we had our first son and so we understood that carrying a delivering a healthy baby was a precious gift and one that many parents don't appreciate. But I grieved the loss of another baby we would never meet. We decided that we would try again. Six months later, we received the news we were expecting again, only to lose it again. This rollercoaster ride continued two more times over the next two years. I remembered knowing I needed to be content with our two beautiful boys but when we picked out our boy's "big climber" for the backyard, I asked the salesman to add a third "baby" swing, just in case. The emotional and physical toll each miscarriage took on my body was becoming too much. I remember breaking down one night and asking God to take away the desire to have another baby and that if it were His will for us to only have two children, I would accept that. I shared with my husband that physical and emotional pain was consuming me and I was headed into a state of depression. We decided together that we would pray about it and if God would allow us to have one more chance, we would take it. We saw fertility specialists, and they told us they couldn't find anything wrong with either one of us. Dreams of a baby girl with ballet slippers filled my nights and the longing wouldn't go away. Our doctor told us we would need help via progesterone shots, which didn't sound fun, but I knew many other couples went through many more difficulties getting pregnant and so be it. We decided we would wait until the Fall so that if I were lucky enough to get pregnant, our baby would be born in the Spring. I knew three children under ten years old would be expensive for daycare so my plan was that I could take the summer off. On Father's Day 1999, as we were celebrating the weekend with our best friends, we learned that we were pregnant again, but while most couples celebrate the "we're expecting" with great joy, in my heart my first thought was how we didn't follow his advice to get the recommended progesterone shots that would ensure a successful pregnancy. As we began our usual weekly checkups, our doctor told us that the baby wasn't developing and that the chances were high I would once again miscarry. We were scheduled to take our first family cruise, on the Disney ship, no less, and the doctors told us we needed to make plans to be airlifted to a local hospital in the Bahamas in the event should miscarry while on the ship. The Sunday before we set sail, we went to the altar and told God that we trusted in Him implicitly. As we returned from this fun filled, memory-making trip, we went to our scheduled weekly appointment and prepared for the worst. After weeks of worrying, we received the incredible news every parent wants that the baby was growing and that he was releasing us back to our regular doctor. In those moments of shock and elation, we thanked God for His goodness and appreciated the gift of life. We knew God had a sense of humor when the nurse told us our due date was 2/29/00. Praise the Lord! We were expecting our third baby and my heart was filled with joy overflowing. The next months were busy with planning for our new addition and when we learned it was a girl, we testified that we had a double blessing! Our daughter arrived on February 27, 2000 and everyone who knew us celebrated with us as they knew the journey we were on and how our faith kept us believing and trusting.

I remember that faith walk like yesterday. Praying for God to provide but not knowing if it wasn't His will. It is hard when praying for His will. It's a very hard place to be. Our human nature justifies all the reasons why it "should be". Why would God not allow us to have another child? But we already were blessed with two. The thoughts never escape your conscious.

I learned during that time that even when our trusting means hoping. And hope can turn into sadness, we must never lose hope. Hope allows us to dream and make plans. And when our dreams and plans don't turn out like we dreamed and hoped for, it can be crushing.

For someone who didn't have a "testimony" a few short years early, I shared this very personal struggle that I had with other women because I knew the pain of loss and the joy of life. What we experienced was nothing short of a miracle. When the doctors told us no, God said yes. He is the Great Healer. Many people had seen His mighty hand at work. But I did not understand what was yet to come.

It was a sunny day when we took our children up to visit my dad, Pepa, on Father's Day in June 2005. Life was good! Or as I would say, "life is as it should be". The words of the song "Blessed be the Name" became very real to me when you spend a lot of time in crisis. Our busy lives were filled with football games and cheerleading with our kids and all the fun things families do. Our family took advantage of special days like these to come together to celebrate being a family. My son and nephew asked if they could stay with my parents for the week since it was summer vacation. When my Tyler came home, he told me how my dad had been coughing and he was very concerned about him. At 10 years old, while they were looking forward to horseback riding and car rides for ice cream with the grandparents, Pepa's cough kept them from doing those things. Doctor appointment after doctor appointment yielded no results so after receiving a call to go to the emergency room on Labor Day, I urged my mom to ask for a lung x-ray. I was shocked when we received the results and was told that my dad had stage 4 lung cancer. I questioned how this could happen when he had quit smoking 15 years earlier. My mom, who just the year before had her aortic valve replaced, continued to smoke yet he was the one who would get lung cancer? Why? How? Our lives were turned upside down. We spent countless days at the hospital for tests and chemotherapy. I prayed for his healing because I thought what a "testimony" of healing he would have. I remember sitting on his bed after he made the decision to end the chemotherapy and his words were, "it's like the song "torn between two lovers". I want to be here with all of you but I'm tired. I'm ready to be with my mom and dad and sister in Heaven". I told my dad, "Dad, you will get to see Jesus, the day I long for". One month later, just six short months after Father's Day, my amazing, beloved and full of life dad, lost his battle to cancer. While the world celebrated Martin Luther King's birthday, our hearts were broken as we had to said goodbye to the man who we all adored. I questioned God. I was angry at God. It wasn't fair. Healing did not come on this side of earth. I remember people telling me that God doesn't waste pain. He uses it for good. But how could losing my dad be used for good? I remember in the midnight hours, while tossing and turning trying to sleep, I could feel God's presence so strongly. As I would cry into my pillow because my heart was broken, I could feel His arms wrapping around me like a soft blanket providing me with a peace that I couldn't understand but could feel. He is truly the God of comfort. When I could hardly drag myself out of bed, He gave me the strength to do it.

A few short months after his passing, I told the leaders of our local community foundation I wanted to use my experience to help other people in my situation. That year we created the "Foundation Angel Program" in his honor to help other families affected by cancer or other life-threatening illness in practical ways by matching them with "angels".

My "testimony" now, included how God can use tragedy for good if we will recognize it. While I knew I couldn't bring my dad back, I could use this experience to help others when they were dealing with their tragedy. Today, this program has served over 750 families in a variety of ways. Yes, God can use something tragic for good.

We often feel we should be spared from pain. We believe if we go to church, we tithe and we pray, that we should be spared from losses and catastrophic events, right? What I learned was that it isn't God that causes these things to happen. It is part of life. In life there are disappointments, accidents, tragedies, broken hearts. It is how we respond to these situations that determines if we will live in fear, sadness or joy.

I choose to live in joy and to turn my grief into something that would honor my father. It wasn't easy but with God's help and guidance, we could help many families and they, in turn, touch us with their quiet strength and resilience.

Six years passed, and my Mother went into the hospital for a second aortic valve replacement. She knew she had to have the surgery and she hoped to have it in September, so she can recover and be ready for Christmas Eve, the one day of the year when all the family would be together. After 3 long weeks struggling for her to recover from a botched surgery, we learned that she was paralyzed from her waist down. Our excitement to have it behind us was replaced with fear of how we could we care for her for the rest of her life in a wheelchair. The tremendous pressure we felt was like a giant weight bearing down on us. While we would do anything for our mom, she needed around the clock care because they also had her on a trachea tube so she could no longer speak. Three long weeks went by and the last surgery to repair a torn trachea tube was completed and we were now planning to bring her to a nursing home where she would have to live for the rest of her life. Shortly after hearing from her doctor that her surgery was successful, while she still in the recovery room, I decided to go to my office to work for a few hours. Within 30 minutes of arriving, I received a call from my sister that my mom was gone. We were left with no answers as to how or why this happened. No last words to say, "I love you, mom". In an instant she was gone. Why God? Why would you take away our mom now? We were prepared to pull together as a family and care for her because even though life was taken away from her as she planned, we were going to be there for her going forward. But now, she was gone, and all we had left was confusion and broken hearts. It was in my grief that I prayed to God to provide peace and comfort to my family. I knew the God who can heal a broken heart as He had for me but now, I begged him to be there for my brothers and sister along with the grandchildren who not only lost their beloved Pepa but also their Meme now. There were no words.

As difficult as it was to move on, life went back to normal. We looked forward to Christmas Eve when we could all be together again. Our time together was more precious now than ever before. On December 4th, I received the phone call that no sibling ever wants to receive. My sister called me to tell me that my brother was found dead of an overdose. As I reeled from the shock of this phone call, I knew I had to be there to hold the family together once again. It had only been a little over 2 months since we buried our mother so the thought that this could be happening to our family was incomprehensible. God, where are you? If you are a loving God how could you allow this to happen to our family? You have taken away our parents and now my younger brother? This is NOT the testimony I wanted. Who would even believe this could be real?

As I went through day after day and night after night, consumed by grief still trying to process the loss of my mom and now my little brother, just two months later, I was numb. It was in the darkest of the night when my heart would physically hurt because of the grief and the pain. It was there I felt Christ's love and comfort in a new way. I could feel his arms wrapped around me and hear in the night's stillness God telling me I would be okay. That they were all home and in no more pain. Grief can feel like you are being swallowed by the deepest pit. It makes you feel as if you cannot breathe. You don't want to laugh because you feel guilty because they no longer are here to have laughter. You feel you shouldn't be here. You think of all the things you wished that they were here to enjoy with you. Every holiday becomes an event you want to miss. Every birthday they miss feels so unfair, surely there was so much they were to experience. Your heart is pulled back out of your chest again when new babies are born, and memories are made because you feel the void left by their absence.

Time went on and in early March, I received the call that my best friend, who had been fighting cancer for the past 10 years was in ICU and they didn't think she would pull through. Not another death. I cannot endure this pain again. Through a miraculous series of unexplained events, I was there by her side when she took her last breath. A young mother with two teenagers, gone. Left behind was her husband and family who looked to me for strength. Because I had already experienced many losses, I felt like God had prepared me for this moment. As I looked at the sorrow in each of their eyes, I was able to draw strength from within that I never knew I had. As I gazed out the window of her hospital room as the snowflakes settled on the window sill and sounds coming from all the machines she was connected to, I felt such a peace.

A peace I had never felt. I knew this beautiful woman whom I had laughed and cried with for so long would no longer be suffering. I thought of my father, my mother and my brother as well as her father, who were waiting on the other side to embrace her. I knew that she would soon be face to face with Jesus. I remembered that conversation I had with my dad when we he told me he did not want any more chemo because he couldn't imagine another day filled with vomiting and wanting to die. I didn't understand it at that time because dying was so final and meant the end. While I believed I would go to Heaven when I died, it wasn't until you are so close to the reality of death it hits you. It's like a thin veil that you can see a glimpse of Heaven through. Vilma went to be with the Lord within just a few hours of my arrival. While I rushed around telling her family they needed to tell her what they wanted to say before it was too late, and while they looked at me with fear, I had a sense of peace. A peace that passed all understanding. I lead them in "Amazing Grace" and a prayer and when the doctor's told her husband that the end was near, he asked me to be there with her. Me? This was a tremendous responsibility but also an honor. As I stood by her bedside stroking her hair and telling her she didn't have to fight anymore, time stood still because at that moment nothing else mattered. As she took her last breath, I clasped her hand and within a few moments I felt life leave her body and she was gone. I had grabbed a rose out of a vase as I entered her room and as I placed the beautiful and fragrant rose on her chest and as she lay on the fresh, white sheets, she looked like Sleeping Beauty. This memory became a memory her family could keep in their hearts forever knowing that she was now running into the arms of Jesus happy, healthy and whole.

With a different perspective of death, I faced the reality that one of my dearest and best friends was no longer there for those phone calls, visits to the Big City and Easter celebrations at Disney. My heart ached for all those that had left me too soon. As always, life went back to normal for everyone but as you face each day ahead, death changes you. It not only makes you realize how precious it is to have time with your loved ones and family, but it also makes you put things in perspective and prioritize what is important. Most people don't think about these things until it is too late. I live with that perspective each day.

September 17, 2015 started off as a normal day. As I showered and was getting ready for work, I received a call from my niece who cried hysterically and told me "mom is gone!". I begged her to stop crying and tell me where she went. She said "No, she's gone! she's dead!". As I sat is disbelief that this could never in a million years be possible, I knew that I needed to get there. As I made the hour-long drive to her home, my thoughts were filled with how, what, why? There was no way that this could be true. I thought maybe this is just a nightmare, but I knew that that was not the case. My baby sister, one who I had loved, supported, fought with and, yes, I'm being honest, hated at times yet loved from the depths of my soul, was gone. The anger, pain, denial, grief was more than I could handle. To this day, even after an autopsy proved it was an overdose, I still can't believe this happened.

To this day, I still am numb and have a very difficult time allowing myself to accept this truth. Even though my little brother and I visited with her in the hospital and she showed signs of a drug addiction, I had no idea in my wildest nightmares that this could ever happen to our family again. Not my brother and my sister. It seemed impossible. But, sadly, it is our reality. I remember many mornings waking up and in those first few seconds of being half awake, half asleep, I would think she was still here. Several years have passed but no counseling can remove the pain and sadness that this caused. There are no answers to why this happened, could we have prevented it or even why she didn't seek any help. It is one of those mysteries I will carry in my heart for as long as I live. When I see her again in Heaven, and I know she is there, I will ask her why. For now, I must rest knowing that she is no longer dealing with the demons that caused her to go down the path of drugs.

I have lost several close friends over the past few years and each time, my first thought and sense of relief is that they knew the Lord. My priority in this world is that I share God's love with those I meet. I try to show His love and mercy to those I see struggling because you don't know what they are going through and if it will be the last time you see them.

There continues to be times when I don't hear from my loved ones and fear sets in. I immediately think the worst. They laugh when they tell me to not over- react and they are okay. But deep down, I always expecting "that" phone call. I've received too many of those calls and the thought it could and will happen again one day

haunts me. 2 Timothy 1:7 tells us that *"God has not given us a spirit of fear and timidity, but of power, love, and self-discipline."* I recognize I must not live in fear and that is something I work on daily. God has taught me to trust in Him and that no matter what trials come my way, He has proven faithful.

Each year I ask God to give me a word. As I prayed for the word for 2019, the word "joy" kept coming into my spirit. I thought about how, for so many years, I did not have joy. For many years as I raised my children working a job that I dreaded, I felt no joy. There was happiness in spending time with my children and husband, living life and making memories that I savor today. But I did not have the real joy that you feel in your heart that makes you want to just laugh out loud with…. well, joy. But over the past few years, as I have experienced trials, I have learned that true joy is not something you own, it's something you receive. It is the hidden treasure that makes you realize that no matter what happens, no matter who hurts you, no matter how many financial struggles you have, it is knowing no matter what, I will be okay. It's knowing when I'm with my family, it may be the last time as I know God can call me home without notice and I want my family to have wonderful memories with me. I want to share my gifts with the world as time is fleeting. I want others who are hurting and feeling "joyless" to know you can have joy! It isn't something you can buy, it is something you live out each day. It is noticing the smallest of God's wonders and the vastness of His creation. It is enjoying a glass of wine, laughter and sometimes even knowing no matter how much work remains to be done, (yes, I struggle often with being a workaholic) the work will still be there tomorrow, and I cannot feel guilty. It is knowing no matter how hard the enemy tries to steal my joy, remind me of my weaknesses or tell me that my future looks hopeless, I have the confidence and promise that joy comes in the morning. It is knowing that although death is all around me, I must look at it as a reminder that we are all given a short time on this beautiful earth and we must make the most of each day. We must LIVE. We are called to be the light to each other in this dark world. Our words affect people and we can speak life or death into them. I choose life. I have created my best life and if I can, as painful as it is, share my trials and tribulations with another person and they are encouraged and inspired to choose life over living in the pain of the past, then I will know I have done what God has called me to do. I promised myself and God that I would turn my tests into my testimony.

I know that my journey ahead will have more tests and there will be people in my life that will hurt me. Yes, there will be unexpected disappointments but no matter where He leads, I have this promise He will never leave or forsake me. I won't sweat the things that have no eternal value other than to distract me from focusing on my blessings. I won't sweat the small stuff, and yes, they are all small stuff!

I have learned that when life leads you down the dark valleys of loss, no matter if it is, losing a limb as in my husband's situation, losing a job, or losing a loved one, how we respond to it that will make all the difference. You must choose joy. As a believer, we find it easy to talk about our faith but when faced with difficulty, we must prove that we have faith. How can we talk about our faith if we don't live it out when we are tested? We would be a hypocrite! We must have complete knowledge He is there. In the muck and the mire of it all. In the messiness of broken relationships and even when we are wronged. God can use all these experiences as opportunities to mold us into the women He has created us to be and we can use our experiences to help someone else.

2nd Corinthians 1:4 reminds us that, *"Who gives us comfort in all our troubles, so that we may others who are in trouble, through the comfort with which we ourselves are comforted by God".*

My favorite Bible verse has been Jeremiah 29:11. I have it on a cross hanging on my wall. It says "For I know the plans I have for you,' declares the Lord, 'plans to prosper you and not to harm you, plans to give you hope and a future.'"

Author and blogger, Mary DeMuth, addresses our misunderstanding of this verse in her post, Jeremiah 29:11 Doesn't Mean What You Think. As she explains, the heart of the verse is "not that we would escape our lot, but we would learn to thrive in the midst of it".

Psalm 139:16 assures me that "All the days ordained for me were written in your book before one of them came to be." This tells me that God already knows what lies ahead for us. The good, the bad, the pain and the joy. And, He will give us a glorious future. Yet as we continue our journey on this earth, as beautiful as it can be but, yet, as fallen as it is, we must hold the truth that that the best growth comes through persevering through trials, not running from them. When we learn perseverance, we find surprising joy. Joy that will take us out of the deepest pit and no matter what, we will be okay. No matter how dark the night, joy comes in the morning.

I often think back on the day I told God I had no testimony. While I have had more than my share of sadness than most people, I have learned that as we live and breathe, no matter what life throws at us, the joys and pain, we have to look at each obstacle as an opportunity to grow and learn. One day your test will become your testimony. Your testimony will become your message. And your message may be the encouragement that someone else will need to get them through their darkest valley and give them hope. Because it is there in the darkest valley, that you will feel the loving arms of Jesus wrapped around you to not only to comfort you but to carry you. I treasure joy now more than ever. There are days when you will feel the tremendous weight of grief but then there are days when joy creeps back in, when you don't expect it.

There are still many nights when I toss and turn thinking of those I lost and the memories we shared, but joy comes in the morning and I remember they are dancing in heaven with my Savior. I remember feeling guilty when I would laugh. You see, grief comes in waves. I told myself I will cry when I need to cry, but I will laugh when I can laugh.

Joy is the feeling in your soul you can't create but we must embrace. Though people can try to steal it, it is ours to keep. We can hold on to it, but it is so much better when we give it away. And when we give it away it will always come back to us bringing us deeper and deeper into a new appreciation for life. Yes, no matter how dark the night, joy does come in the morning and brings the promise of a new day to make memories that I will cherish always.

Liz Brewer

As a John Maxwell Certified Trainer and Coach, Liz teaches and shares her experience in leadership to help others increase their influence both personally and professionally. Since 2015, Liz has been hosting monthly "Connections" events to bring women together for inspiration and personal growth. Liz is a featured author in the book, "Yes, God" to be published in April and also facilitates Mastermind groups.

Liz Brewer has enjoyed a successful career in real estate in the Greater Brandon area as a Realtor and Mortgage Lender for the past 32 years. Liz and her son, Jeff, are "The Brewer Team" and Team Leaders of the Brandon branch of Excel Realty offering real estate services to their clients.

Liz has been using her vast knowledge in real estate to recruit, train and coach real estate agents. She is the founder of "Realtor Up & Running", a training program she created to train new agents on the foundational skills they need to be successful and hosts Realtor Bootcamps.

Liz is very passionate about our community and has served as the Executive Director of the Greater Brandon

Community Foundation since 2014 and served as a volunteer since it started in 2004. She created the Angel Program in 2006 after the death of her father to lung cancer to bring together businesses and individuals to serve local families affected by a life-threatening illness or catastrophic event. To date, the Angel Foundation has helped over 750 families in crisis.

Liz was the Honorary Mayor of Brandon in 2014-2015 which is won by the person who raises the most money in the month of June for their charities. Liz and her Campaign Team were able to give $33,000 to three local charities in our community.

It is Liz's passion to serve others through her God-given gifts of training, coaching and connecting to help others create their best life.

Renee Otiende
Yes, God!

Have you ever seen a video on Facebook or YouTube of someone who is ready to take the leap and bungee jump off the side of a bridge or mountain? There are normally 2 kinds of people: the first person is excited about the leap – they are pumped! They are ready to take the leap and when they jump off, they scream – not a scream of fear but of pure joy and adrenaline relief. Then you have the second person – you know this person – nervous, holding onto the instructor, and unwilling to jump off. The second person looks back at the group they came with saying "I don't think I can do this!" They look at the instructor – the person who told them what to do, the person who prepared them for this leap – and they say, "I don't think I am ready." Sometimes in those videos the instructor has to say, "Listen, you know what to do and what to expect. Take the leap or get off of the platform." And then then they take the leap and they scream too but their scream is a mixture of adrenaline relief, excitement and fear. Sometimes you get to see the 2nd person after the jump and you might hear them say one of 2 things, "I can't wait to do that again" or "I will never do that again."

If I am honest, I wish I was like the first person when God has asked me to take a leap of faith. I wish that I immediately jump when he said jump and enjoy the ride. But the truth is I am more like the second person. Looking at God questioning if this leap makes sense – looking to my friends for their encouragement and agreement with this leap – screaming along the way with a mixture of emotions: fear, excitement and joy.

As I have walked through making faith leaps in my life, what I call a faith journey, the one thing I have to always remember is my faith journey is not about how small or big the faith leap or how I well I made the leap but that I made the leap. Sometimes you have to make the leap – sometimes it will be graceful and other times you might be a little less than elegant. God does not require perfection – he requires obedience. He has done more with my obedience than he has ever done with my "perfection".

I have just finished making another faith leap. In 2011, I graduated from seminary with my masters in Christian Education. I had the desire to equip and prepare people for Christian missions but when I graduated, I had a toddler, a newborn, student loans and I did not see how God would provide for us on a ministry salary. So, I continued to work in corporate America and then in September 2013 I was laid off. One of the biggest banks in the world was closing down our site and we would have to look for a job elsewhere. Some of my friends asked, "So, now are you going to serve in ministry full time?" The thought had not crossed my mind to find a job in ministry. And when I thought about pursuing a job in ministry the doubts flooded in – there aren't many African Americans serving in missions, you have no experience in this field, how will your family survive on a ministry salary, and the list goes on.

So, I looked for other jobs and then in December 2013 I received an email from a dear friend and mentor who worked for a Christian mission's agency. She sent me an email with a job opening and the subject of the email was: Would you be open to part-time work? The answer to that question was NO. I already knew a ministry salary would be less than the salary I received before but now part-time! But when I read the position description, I knew the job was perfect for me. After talking with my husband and a few friends I applied for the position. In December 2013 I was offered the position and started in January 2014. I absolutely loved serving, equipping and sending people to the missions' field. I loved the organization I served with and the people I got to serve with every day. Over the next four years I would be promoted twice, and God provided for us in such miraculous ways. It was a dream come true – a dream I had given up on 7 years prior.

So, to my surprise in 2018 I got the impression it was time to leave and pursue another dream. I took months to verbalize what I was feeling. I was honestly hoping that the Lord would take this impression away. But he did not, and it only grew stronger. I always wanted to be a teacher since I was little. But my path in life did not take me down the road of teaching or training professionally. My current job in ministry allowed me to train but not very much compared to my other daily activities. Whenever I could be trained or taught, I took advantage of it. I enjoyed training so much and even taking courses on the side and researching training theories and techniques. I wondered and ask God is the next leap for me … becoming a corporate trainer. But doubts creeped in again … "I have never done this before, who would hire me?", "I have never been to school for this who would hire me?", "Do I have the skills set to be good at this job?", and many more.

Despite all the doubts in November 2018 I informed the ministry I would begin to look for another job in the new year. Now you may think, "Why did you let your current employer know you were leaving before you had another job lined up?" There were 2 reasons: the first was I wanted to leave the ministry well leaving, and the second was I had a test to pass. Let me explain the ministry I served with depended on me to perform several functions. At the time I did not have an apprentice or someone that was learning my job. I knew if I gave them the customary 2-4 week notice when resigning from a position the transition may not be very smooth for them. Although I knew that God was calling me elsewhere, I also knew that all of my work is unto Him. The second reason is I felt I was being tested. I felt like the Lord was asking, "Will you trust me to provide even when you don't see how?" "Will you take the leap even when the path is not clear?"

As promised in January 2019 I turned in my resignation letter and I applied for corporate trainer positions. Both decisions were hard. It was one thing to say I was leaving, but it was much harder to write the resignation letter and turn it in. There was a part of me that was saying, "This is crazy!" but there was a bigger part of me that was screaming, "Trust God!" Now it was time to update my resume and apply for positions. Those doubts from before came back again - that voice in my head - "How are you going to put a resume together when you don't have anything to put on it?" Around this same time, I was praying and fasting with my church and during one morning of praying, God said, "Just finish the resume. I will put it in the right hands if you put it out there." So, I finished my resume and applied for jobs.

By the end of January, I only heard from one legitimate company and they wanted to interview me for a corporate trainer position. One of my mentors said, "It only takes one." By February 8, I had completed 1 phone interview, 3 formal interviews, 1 mock presentation, and I was offered the role as a corporate trainer for a large financial institution in the Dallas Fort Worth area!

As you read my faith leap you may think, "How did you know what move to make?", "That sounds to simple, it can't be that easy." , "How was your spiritual life when you made these decisions?" There were 3 elements that were a part of my daily life when I made this faith leap and I believe it has to be a part of all our lives if we want to say "Yes!" to God. The 3 elements are: God's word, prayer and community.

God's Word

"Your word is a lamp unto my feet and a light to my path."
- Psalm 119:105

The funny thing is God's word doesn't tell me explicitly what move to make next. Instead, God's word checks my heart. We all have dreams; some come from our earthly desires and others come from God. Reading God's word reveals the source of my dreams: worldly dreams or God-given dreams. When I realize the source of my dreams, I know what dreams to release and what dreams to pursue. Jeremiah 17:9 tells us, "The heart is deceitful above all things, and desperately sick; who can understand it?" My heart is where I have hidden hurts, selfish expectations and personal vows. When I have an encounter with God's word daily the hidden things are illuminated and checked. I am forced to deal with the parts that are ungodly and when I deal with them the ungodly dreams are dealt with.

Once the ungodly desires start to be removed the God-placed dreams can be seen more clearly. Once you know the dreams God has given you - you pursue them with all that you have. You pursue them when it doesn't make sense to the world. You pursue them despite the doubts in your head. You pursue them because the God of the universe has an assignment for you to accomplish.

God's word not only directs my path, but it also provides me with encouragement and hope as I pursue God-given dreams. I think we would all agree it is difficult enough understanding what dreams are earthly versus godly. But it is a whole other endeavor to walk in the pursuing of that dream.

Ephesians 2:10 says, *"For we are his workmanship", created in Christ Jesus for good works, which God prepared beforehand, that we should walk in them."* As we read the first part of this verse, *"For we are his workmanship",* understand that we are God's children, adopted into His family, co-heirs with Jesus Christ, no longer orphans, and we have all the rights and responsibilities as His children. This ought to make us walk taller and confident despite what may come our way because we are a child of the King.

Then the verse says, "created in Christ Jesus for good works". Have you ever really thought you were created for good works? We were created for a good purpose and our God-given dreams are a part of those good works. We were created for this! All of your life, the good and the bad, is a part of this moment.

No one else can do the good work "which God prepared beforehand" for us to do. And God is not making this plan for us on the fly or as He goes. He prepared this for us beforehand, before the beginning of time, before we were formed in our mother's' womb, we were on His mind and He decided how our life would bring Him the most glory. Our lives have not been a mistake - we may have made mistakes, but they were not a surprise to God. He knew how He would use all of us for His purpose.

Lastly, "that we should walk in them", God did not prepare good works for us before the beginning of time for us to only write them in our journals, ponder over them, hide them, or get buy-in from the world. The bible says for us to "walk in them"; walk is an action verb and our response requires action. Regarding the faith step God is telling us to make it means we have to take action: update the resume, interview someone who has the job you want, take the college course, get the certification, apply for the business loan, ask that person to mentor you, schedule a meeting with the investor, make the appointment with the counselor. Take Action!

One last thought about God's word, I have to check my posture. There have definitely been seasons when I am reading God's word and it just doesn't make sense, I don't understand how it applies to my life or I don't "feel" anything when I read it. The truth is it is more about my posture during those times - prideful and approaching God's word as an item to check off my daily to do list. If I only see reading God's word as just an item on my to-do list, I have a heart problem. I don't see how desperately fragile I am and how I need God's word like I need air to breathe. When I see myself rightly and remember that I desperately need to have an encounter with the God of the universe the bible always has something for me. He has lovingly provided His word and every time I am exposed to it there is something for me, for that day and for His glory. When I read the bible with that posture there is loving conviction of sins that should result in confession, application for living, comfort, encouragement that help me pursue the dreams He has for me to accomplish for His glory.

Prayer

The purpose of prayer is not to get what you want; the goal of prayer is to discern what God wants, what God wills. But if your prayer is in the will of God, then it is backed by the full authority of the King and His kingdom.

~Mark Batterson, *Draw the Circle*

For a long time, I did not understand the purpose of prayer and how prayer works. My belief was that I was going to God to ask Him to change His mind about something or to make something happen. But I couldn't reconcile how an all-knowing, all-powerful God would change His divine will, set before the beginning of time based on how well or how often I prayed. So, for a long time my prayer life was scattered, sometimes non-existent and fruitless.

But God does not give up on us and he continues to pursue a relationship with us. Because of His grace, through His word, sermons, books and other resources I changed my view of prayer. As my view of prayer changed, I approached prayer as communication with God instead of "rubbing a genie bottle". Now in the beginning it was a more one-way communication, me talking to God, freely sharing my thoughts, feelings, fears, worries, and doubts. I also would share my hopes, dreams, wishes and desires. There was something about sitting in God's presence, being fully known and experiencing his peace, grace and abundant love. I never felt condemned for what I confessed or how I felt.

Then my prayer life evolved into a 2-way communication. So, here's a question you might have, "Do you hear an audible voice from God?" For me it has not been an audible voice but more like impressions, thoughts that come from what seems like nowhere, and also loving reminders of biblical truths. During these times of prayer, that is where God gives me impressions of people to pray for, people to help, sin to stop, changes I need to make and yes, God-inspired dreams to pursue.

It is through prayer and God's word I can see what move to make next. I have to remind myself that it is not about the size of the move but that I make the move. When I got the impression, it was time to pursue a new dream it was during prayer that God encouraged me to reach out to a training professional. I did not understand that she would help me prepare for my interview and presentation. It was during my time in prayer where I found peace about sending in my resignation letter when I didn't have another job. It was during my prayer time that God strongly told me to finish my resume. I did not understand that He would provide a job for me a month later. It was during my time in prayer that God told me to pray for the people that would interview me and that I would have an opportunity to encourage them. I had no idea that I would have a 45-minute interview with a senior executive about how to be a self-aware leader and heal from past hurts. Prayer is about positioning myself to hear from God so He will get the glory through my faith leaps.

Community

Better is open rebuke than hidden love.

"Wounds from a friend can be trusted, but an enemy multiplies kisses. " ~Proverbs 27:5-6

My community is my inner circle of family and friends. My husband, mom, best-friend for over 30 years and friends I that I have met in the last 10 years are all in my community. These people are all different; they are artists, caretakers, teachers, counselors, blue-collar workers and lawyers. They all think completely different about some ideas and agree on others. Although they are different and the origins of our connection are diverse, they have qualities in common. They are actively pursuing a closer relationship with the Lord, self-aware, honest with me and love me no matter what. A community with these qualities is essential when you are making a faith leap.

Your community will probably look very different from my inner circle, but we all need a close group of people when we are making a faith leap. We were not created to live in isolation, and we were definitely not created to decide in isolation. When it comes time to make a faith leap, your community is vital. Your community provides a prayer covering, confirmation, encouragement and accountability.

I am confident my inner circle is interceding on my behalf before our heavenly Father. I know in the same way He gives me impressions and people to pray for; God is doing the same for them. There were moments when they prayed for my interview and I felt perfect peace. Sometimes I did not feel clear direction, and they prayed for clarity. Sometimes my community prayed for me because God gave them the prayer to pray not because I asked.

My community sees qualities and gifts in me I may not see in myself. They sometimes see the dream before I do. It is an encouragement for someone to remind you of your God-given abilities and spur you on to see what God has in store for you. I love it when a friend calls at just the right time when I needed their encouragement.

They can also see my blind spots. We have to share our decisions with our community, and it may be hard when they confirm your decision. Confirmation serves like a "checks and balances" system. You may have good intentions, but your community is looking out for what you may have missed. You are not seeking approval from the world; you going to your inner circle to make the best God-honoring decision. My community is seeking the Lord on my behalf and they can see things I may not know of. We must be open for our friends to speak truth in our lives and create a safe place for them to share with us.

Our inner circles not only pray for our faith leap, confirm our faith leap and encourage our faith leap; our community hold us accountable to our faith leaps. I will not be perfect at anything - making a faith leap is included in anything. When my doubts overwhelm me, I experience a setback and I get discouraged, not only does my community encourage me but they hold me accountable to get back on track.

As you see God illuminate your path and you see the faith leap produce fruit: you get the job, you see breakthrough in your marriage, you get the business loan, or you conduct your first seminar. When you see the dream becoming reality, I want to warn you of 3 items: distractions, pride, and ungratefulness.

Distractions

We have a real enemy and his name is Satan. Since the beginning of time he has tried to usurp the glory that belongs to God for himself. He knows how this story ends and the Lord is victorious but that does not stop him from trying to knock us off course. The enemy first tries to knock us off course by trying to make us doubt God's plan for us. But through God's word, prayer, and community we can be very sure of the direction God has for us. When the enemy knows that we are certain in our path forward he still doesn't give up. That is when he brings distractions.

Distractions come and can cause you to take your eye off the goal. Distractions really can get you off course. You and your husband are doing well and then all of sudden you are in an argument - one of those arguments that last more than a day. You wonder to yourself, "How did we get here? What is going on? What happened we were good yesterday?" Or some problem at work comes out of nowhere or a family member gets sick or then your child has an issue at school, or you don't feel well. When we look at the things individually, unconnected, we might say, "Wow, there is so much going on right now!" Distractions can come as big situations, but they can also come as small things. When I was right in the middle of making my faith leap my daughter fell and chipped her front tooth. Nothing major but it was enough to distract me. Our adversary knows when He sees a determined child of God that he may not make you doubt God, but He causes enough stuff around us to take place that it gets you your mind off what the Lord told you to do.

When we step out and make the faith leap, we have to be clear that we are at war. The bible says we are always at war and when we make a faith leap it can feel like active combat. Active combat is when the enemy is coming at us from all directions and using all the weapons He has in his arsenal. Active combat is where he tests are full armor. He is waiting to see if we are going to use the armor or if we are going to forget that we are in a spiritual battle and instead use our physical weapons. That is where distractions mess you up because instead of using the weapons for spiritual warfare, we use the weapons for physical/earthly warfare: my logic, my feelings, a good self-help book, some video on the internet. Instead of taking notice to all that is going on around you and remember that the Lord has called you to make a faith leap. A leap that will give Him all the glory. When I recognize that I am in a spiritual battle I need to put away my earthly weapons and use my spiritual ones: God's word and prayer. Yes, we will address the argument, take care of the chipped tooth and help the sick family member. But we will not allow it to overwhelm us and distract us from the Lord is calling us to do.

Pride

When I received the exciting news on February 8 to tell me I was offered the job the hiring manager said, "We think you have a lot to offer the team. There is so much the team will be able to learn from you." When I called my friends to let them know the good news, some said, "I knew you would get." Others said, "You are going to be so good at that position." When I told a fellow co-worker that I was leaving and the area I was going to, she said, "That is no surprise. You are a natural." When I thought about my new opportunity, the thought crossed my mind, "I prayed so well, that's why I received this job." For a brief moment I began to believe my own "press report", I began to think it was through my skills that I obtained the job - I wanted to get the credit not God.

Pride always wants to put the glory on myself instead of God. Pride can sometimes be very subtle by simply having your internal reflections be on yourself instead of God and how He wants to use you at this new assignment. This is why it is important to have God's word, prayer and your community along the way. God's word will remind and convict you when pride is showing up in your life. Honestly for me it can creep up all the time. God's divine providence knows exactly what scripture I need on a particular day. Prayer especially during my quiet time is when I can hear from the Holy Spirit and receive His loving conviction. Once I recognized that I was becoming prideful about my faith leap I have to share that with my community so that they can be aware of my struggle and loving call me out on it when they see it in me. I have to be diligent to examine my heart and deal with pride as soon as I see it in myself.

Ungratefulness

There is a quote that says, "Expectations are premeditated resentments." I have to remember that my heart is deceitful and even a God-given gift can be tarnished by my expectations. In January, during my prayer time I felt led to pray these specific prayers, "Lord, please provide a job in training that challenges me, provides financially for my family in February." So, when I received the call on January 16 for a phone interview as a Corporate Trainer, my response was "Thank you Lord." When I received the email for an in-person interview, my response was, "Thank you Lord." When He sent a friend in training across my path to help me prepare for my interview my response was, "Thank you Lord!" When I received the email for a final interview my response was, "Thank you Lord!" When He provided a training guru to coach me through my final interview and presentation for free my response was, "Thank you Lord!!" After I felt like the final interview went really well, my response was, "Thank you Lord!!" When I was offered the job, my response was, "THANK YOU LORD!!!" When I was provided the offer and heard about the benefits, my response was, "THANK YOU LORD! Thank you for providing and hearing my prayers." When I realized that I had miscalculated my current salary and the offer I accepted was actually less than my current salary, my response was, "Wait a minute Lord. This is not what I asked for. How is this providing for my family." Although I made the prayer has holy as I could my heart expected something much different. I wanted a significant raise in my salary and once I did not get what I expected I looked at God's gift with disdain. How often have I looked at the Lord's gifts with contempt and disrespect - simply put ungrateful?

To avoid the path of ungratefulness, we have to remember our position and the Lord's position. Our point a view is from the singular point in time. We cannot see anything the lies ahead. Our perspective is limited. God has an eternal perspective that exists outside of time. We have to believe that God's ways and plans are better than any plan we can put together. The lower salary for me is still in the middle of God's plan for me and those plans are not to harm me but to give me hope and a future. We have to trust the Lord and gladly accept the gifts he gives us because that is what is best for us.

My faith journey has never been easy it has required total dependence on the Lord, His word, His timing and His provision. But it is the best place to be, knowing God has provided through His word, His presence and His people. So, take the leap and enjoy the journey!

Renee Otiende

Renee Otiende is a lover of Jesus, wife, mother, trainer and now author. Renee Otiende has been equipping people in a variety of settings from banking to religious non-profits for over 10 years. She has a bachelor's degree in Industrial Engineering and a master's degree in Christian Education from Dallas Theological Seminary. She is the wife of Austin and mother to Amani and AJ. Renee especially enjoys sharing her story with people to encourage them to live out their unique purpose.

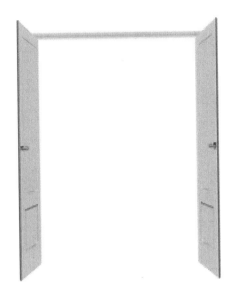

Pastor RichEtta Weathersbee
Yes, God!

Each of us has a journey that God has taken us on. There are moments that occur along that journey that really helped to shape and define who we are. Share one of those Yes, God moments you have encountered, where you had to trust Him without knowing all the steps.

My Yes God moment came in February 2012. I was determining if I would stay in my marriage or dissolve it. I was tired, worn out, and hurting. I wanted all the pain to stop, so I could have joy and peace in my life.

How did you develop your faith when it seemed like nothing was going right in your life? Share a situation where you had to develop your faith walk.

I traveled to Flint, Michigan in February 2012 to preach for a church revival as, I was the keynote speaker. Yes, I was a minister during this time of unhappiness in my marriage. Yet, unbeknownst to me, The Lord would spoke directly into my heart. God led me to preach a sermon titled, "Bend but don't Break!" The passage came from the Book of Luke 13:10-17. This passage spoke of Jesus' teaching in one of the synagogues on the sabbath. I want to share verses 11-13 which states,

"And, behold, there was a woman which had a spirit of infirmity eighteen years, and was bowed together, and could in no wise lift up herself. And when Jesus saw her, he called her to him, and said unto her, Woman, thou art loosed from thine infirmity. And he laid his hands on her: and immediately she was made straight, and glorified God."

Within, this passage I recognized that Jesus didn't give the specific infirmity of this woman, which spoke volumes because we all have some kind of infirmity in our lives that can cause us to become bowed together. If we stay in it that infirmity the consequences will eventually leave us in a crippled or dark place. That is exactly where I was at in my life in February 2012. I had spent 23 years in a marriage I was miserable in and could not see the light at the end of the tunnel. At that time, I was placing the blame of the failure in our marriage on my husband, but God showed me the infirmities I was carrying. When God showed me → ME and my past Infirmities:

I was an adulterer who lied to keep the appearance of an honest wife. I was not a tither, yet I would ask the congregation to trust God with their tithes, and I did not have a solid prayer life, but I would pray for others. Wow! I figured it all out by myself, I did not give God, "My Yes!"

Please do not confuse my lack of giving God my yes, with accepting Christ as my Lord and personal savior. I accepted Jesus Christ as my Lord and personal savior in 1995. I accepted Him because I needed Him as Lord over my life and I knew that I could not make it to heaven without Him. So, yes, I was saved during this time, but I was not faithful to His call on my life. Let me share a couple of the clichés that made it easy for me to continue in my Infirmities:

I heard the following cliché from some Christians in my past, "The Lord does not need us we need Him!" Please understand, I understood perfectly what the preacher was saying when making that comment, but I used it as my scapegoat to work/honor God less. Many people may read about some infirmities I had going on in my life and wonder, "How could she be a preacher and do those type of things?" Well, allow me to answer that question for you with Cliché #2, I said to myself, "Everyone have a sin they need to be delivered from!" I also took parts of scriptures to make my point such as, Ecclesiastes 7:20,

"For there is not a just man upon earth, that doeth good, and sinneth not." I took that passage out of the context in which it was exegetically intended for and said, "There is no perfect person!" I felt as if those clichés vindicated me. In all actuality I was in a, "Consequence state of Being" in my life. My infirmities weighed me down to a point that I was bowled over and could not lift myself up.

My bending caused placed me in a perfect position that was on my knees asking the Lord to create in me a new heart and a right spirit. I asked the Lord to forgive me for all of my sins and transgressions. I asked the Lord to show me →"ME". I was so busy focusing on the hurt I had received from others I became numb to hurt. I have a clearer understanding of the cliché "Hurt people Hurt people".

How did you stay motivated in a season where patience, faith and trust had to be exercised?

I did not want to continue to dishonor God by not going to the appointed place He would have me preach and teach His word. But inwardly I felt a pain that only the Lord could heal. I asked God, "How can I preach and teach your Word if I am guilty by your Word?" I heard God say "It's time for you to repent and say, "Yes to my Will and Yes to my Way." Before I could minister, I had to empty myself out through fasting and prayer. This was the beginning of my, "Yes God!"

As I preached the Word of God at the revival in Flint, Michigan, I heard God say during this sermon, "It's ok to bend just don't break!" See, my bending came from being hard-headed, stubborn, selfish, an adulteress, and not obeying who the Lord called and chose me to be. My bending caused me to have a spiritual emptiness, physical pain, and years of frustration. Yes, you heard me right. My infirmities caused my previous consequences. During this sermon the Lord God laid me out prostrate on the floor. I cried out to God and said, "Right here, right now, my answer is Yes!" Some thought I was simply laid out in the spirit as they waved fans over me. However, what they did not see happening in the spiritual realm was the Lord touched me and said, "You are loosed from your infirmity!" I want you to understand that In my bending I refused to break by giving up and throwing in the towel. The truth of that moment was the realness of my walk and talk had just begun. I got up running, praising, crying, and thanking God for Jesus. "Yes, God!"

I always knew that the Lord could use anyone or anything to preach and teach His Word throughout the nation. I am so blessed that He not only called, but he chose me. I told the Lord, "Send me Lord, I'll Go!" Yes, God! I could only keep repeating the same scripture repeatedly which is, John 8:36, which states, *"If the Son therefore shall make you free, ye shall be free indeed."*

The great thing about God is that He is forgiving, merciful, and full of Grace. The moment that the Lord set me free helped me stop judging my husband. It made me see clearer the man of God that Jesus placed to oversee our family.

I finally understood what I had to go back home and do. I had to ask my husband for his forgiveness; I had to learn how to be submissive; I had to change my thinking; I had to learn how to love myself to love my man of God. I asked the Lord to show me how to love my man of God.

My, Yes God! was for my marriage and family. Once I gave my infirmities to the Lord, I felt a shift in my life. Now, God could use me in a major way. I felt a newfound love for my husband because I said, "Yes, God!" I arrived back home from preaching the revival in Flint, Michigan on February 29th, 2012 (It was Leap Year) ← Don't miss that! While traveling back home I heard the Lord say "Daughter, I'm proud of you and I am about to bless you and it will be unimaginable."

Once I arrived back to Dallas, Texas my husband was there at the airport to pick me up. When I saw him, my heart leaped. I could not wait to make love to my man of God on that day. I found out less than 2 months later that I was pregnant at the age of 44. I gave birth on November 8th, 2012 (The number 8 represents New Beginnings) to our 5th child together and we named her Jade Chanel Weathersbee. That was 3 weeks before my 45th Birthday. On April 15th, 2019, My husband and I will celebrate 30 years of marriage together. We will continue to Make it Last Forever.

What scriptures, books, or resources do you recommend using when you are looking to grow in your walk with God?

In conclusion, I will end my, Yes, God! Chapter with the end passage of Luke 13: 14-17 and summation:

"And the ruler of the synagogue answered with indignation, because that Jesus had healed on the sabbath day, and said unto the people, There are six days in which men ought to work: in them therefore come and be healed, and not on the sabbath day.

15 The Lord then answered him, and said, Thou hypocrite, doth not each one of you on the sabbath loose his ox or his ass from the stall, and lead him away to watering?

16 And ought not this woman, being a daughter of Abraham, whom Satan hath bound, lo, these eighteen years, be loosed from this bond on the sabbath day?
17 And when he had said these things, all his adversaries were ashamed: and all the people rejoiced for all the glorious things that were done by him.

The Lord answered the synagogue leader by calling him a hypocrite, because he followed the Laws when he felt like it but did not follow Him. I had to learn not to worry about what others would think or speak negatively about me. I continue to trust that the Lord will fight my battles. I will allow no one to send me away without receiving what they have for me. In order for me to have been released from my infirmities I had to step back and look at myself. I am so blessed to be called a daughter of Abraham. I am so blessed that the Lord released me from my infirmities that I had carried for over 18 years in my marriage. I am so glad I finally said, "Yes, God!" The Lord gave me the following instructions in the sermon He had me to preach on in Flint, Michigan and I want to share them with you.

Remain in Christ no matter what happens in my life and continue to make it to the church house.

1. The Lord saw me and called me forward.
2. I had to Move out of my Infirmities and into His loving arms.
3. The Lord placed His hands on me because I am His.
4. Never look back to use the past against my husband or myself.
5. Once the Lord set me free, "I Accepted it and Continuously give Him Praise!"
6. I surrendered all.

Pastor RichEtta Weathersbee

Senior Pastor Rich Etta Weathersbee is from Flint, Michigan but currently resides in Allen, Texas. She is the daughter of Deacon Adell Henderson Sr. (Deceased) and Bobbie Henderson-Payne (Deceased). She is married to Deacon Cordell Weathersbee Sr. (30 years) and through their union they have five beautiful children Cordell II, Coretta (Deceased), Shaunice, Le Tasha, and Jade. She is a U.S. Navy Veteran serving 13 years Active Duty and 4 years Reserves.

Pastor Rich Etta has completed two Master Degrees at Dallas Baptist University in Christian Ministries - Chaplaincy (MACM) 2012 and Christian Education (MACE) 2010. She received her Bachelor of Arts and Science Degree in Interdisciplinary Studies/Communications at Dallas Baptist University (2006) and received her Associates Degree in Computer Networking from ITT Technical Institute (2003). She also completed 2 years of Residency (8 Units) of Clinical

Pastoral Education at Baylor University Medical Center where she served 8.5 years as the Regional Staff Chaplain overseeing 8 Baylor Scott & White Emergency Hospitals located in Aubrey, Murphy, Rockwall, Keller, Burleson, Mansfield, Grand Prairie, and Colleyville Texas.

Pastor Rich Etta received her Ecclesiastical Endorsement and serves as an Endorsed Chaplain for the Baptist General Convention of Texas under the leadership of Dr. Bobby Smith (Texas Endorser). She is certified in the following areas: Critical Incident Stress Management (CISM), Applied Suicide Intervention Skills Training (ASIST), Certified Chaplain Coach, and National Organization for Victim Assistance (NOVA).

Pastor Rich Etta received her ministerial license while attending Piney Grove Baptist Church (Virginia Beach, VA) under the leadership of Pastor Charles A. Vinson (1999). She was ordained at Fellowship Baptist Church (2006) currently known as Fellowship Christian Center Church located in Allen, Texas under the leadership of Dr. W.L Stafford, Sr. She was installed and serves as Senior Pastor of Breaking of Bread Church located in Richardson, Texas, by Bishop DD Hayes and Co-Pastor Cheryl Hayes at Gospel Inspirational Fellowship Tabernacle, Ft Worth, Texas (2013). She is also an Associate Chaplain at Dallas Fort Worth Airport. Pastor Rich Etta is the President of Rhema International Fellowship of Churches (RIFC) Women's Department under the Leadership of Overseer Bishop Eric Lloyd and Evangelist Shenita Lloyd, Harper Woods, MI.

Pastor Rich Etta is a Published Author, Award Winning Internet Radio Talk Show Host at Fish Bowl Radio Network, CEO/Founder/President of N2NE (In Tune) Youth Mentoring Program, Inc. 501(c) 3 Non-Profit organization, and CEO/Founder/Publisher of

N2NE (In Tune) Youth Magazine located in Richardson, Texas

Colette Huxtable
Yes, God!

Each of us has a journey that God has taken us on. There are moments that occur along that journey that really helped to shape and define who we are. Share one of those Yes, God moments you have encountered, where you had to trust Him without knowing all the steps.

I walked my journey with inviting God into it and believed that was how I was supposed to do life. I had the privilege of seeing some amazing faith filled people doing life differently. It moved me so much that I opened my heart to God in a way I had never done before and I told God that I would stop dictating my direction and I would follow his direction. That positioned me to learn how to listen to God and to look for where he was working and moving so that I could follow that direction. I also had to wrestle with my belief system if I believed if I left my path to God, would He answer and guide me? Once I solidified that I believed God for that, then even when he was silent for a time or when circumstances appeared negative, I could trust that God was in the midst of them.

One thing I have experienced in my walk with God is that he loves to take something I would never ever choose on my own and ask me to walk in that direction. I find it almost comical how often he does that, and the best part is that when I completely surrender my heart to lay down my own opinions and thoughts on the matter, I find joy and excitement in moving into God's choice. It fascinates me how I can sit with God and listen for his heart on a matter and ask him to change my heart to desire what He wants for me. Every single time he has answered that request.

The biggest moment for me was I have always, and I mean always, said I never wanted to be a business owner. I have an extremely creative husband and he comes up with inventive ideas for products and I would say, "Good luck with that" and wish him well on his adventure of making something come to fruition. He is the stereotypical visionary, so implementation always hindered him from moving forward. I refused to help him implement. That would mean going into business so nope! God strategically placed a role model in my life, and she had such an open and different heart on the matter. She was living out partnering with her spouse in the very area I was saying I will not. I decided I would stop being stubborn and listen to God on the matter. I wanted to see if he would like me to do something different. Of course, he did! He put on my heart to apply for an entrepreneurial program through a Christian business school that would take a year to complete. I applied, was accepted and started within a few months' time.

I was enjoying learning as all of it was completely new to me. The thing I loved the most was it had me seek God and it used biblical principles, which definitely helped keep my interest. One assignment they gave was to pray for God's vision for your business. I was going to help my husband with a business, but I sat down and fervently prayed that God would give me vision. Vision he did! He gave me a vision for ME to start a company. I could not believe that is what he was showing me, and I wanted it. I wanted this vision he placed before me and it made me excited and because I sought him and he answered me, even though it wasn't what I expected, I truly believed him for that vision.

From the moment I saw the picture, I held on to it no matter how crazy it seemed at the time.

His vision he showed me was for a coffee roasting company that would be in a building on my property. I was passionate about good coffee and that is about all the qualifications I had to start. I had to share with my husband this new idea and what I felt God was calling me to and I am so grateful he was open. It all started there. It started with me meditating on the vision God gave me and as I continued in the business school, I would gear all the learning to how it would relate to the coffee roasting business. Near the end of the schooling I found a week long intensive roasting course in another state and asked my husband if he would support me taking that step. He said yes, so I booked it and off I went to step in with no knowledge but a heart to learn. I loved it! It was scary and a bit intimidating but when I got through that part, it was invigorating and exciting and I knew I would love roasting coffee.

During the course of the online program I had also gotten pregnant with my fourth child. I was working as a Registered Nurse part time and in my heart, I felt God was calling me out of nursing to pursue coffee and to be at home with my family. I had to wrestle with who am if I am not a nurse. What does that say about me? He said I am his and that he chose me. That means more to me that any title. One of my RN friends asked about me keeping my license as a backup because we worked so hard for it. I know God had me go into nursing for a purpose. I grew personally and professionally, and I learned leadership along with many other life skills. Nursing school was a difficult journey, but

I don't need a backup plan with God. I am willing to go back into nursing and I am willing to stay out of nursing. I am free to follow God in my career where ever he calls me, and it is such a freeing thing to be in that place because I believe God has his best set before me. To date, after going on maternity leave, I have not gone back to nursing.

Four months after my son was born, I started looking for a roaster and getting set up. The process getting a roasting house and roaster took months. God was even so generous to help me find a mentor to learn all the ins and outs of my machine and the business of roasting. It has taken a year and a half from receiving the vision to manifesting the vision. There were many small moments of things not going the way I felt they should go. One instance was the placement of the roasting house, had we put in the permit fifteen days earlier we could have had the location where we originally desired it.

God gave me a dream the night before I found out that news. In the dream He showed me how important the words I speak are and the power of my tongue. That day I found out the news my flesh wanted to complain and be sad, but I knew not to speak anything negative out of my mouth but to proclaim God has a plan and a solution. I believe speaking agreement for where God was directing me allowed me to be where I am right now. The solution came and it ended up being better than the original spot I had in mind. I am still following him step by step believing him for completing the work he started in me.

How did you develop your faith when it seemed like nothing was going right in your life? Share a situation where you had to develop your faith walk.

I was newly remarried, and God was moving me from captivity of the old into journeying fearlessly with him. My past was definitely trying to cling to me to tell me I couldn't be anything except all the things I had done. God was pursuing me fervently with his transformative love to tell me I am not any of those things and that he removed all that sin from me. I was free to be who He called me to be. During that time of learning the truth of what God was telling me, I had to contend with my past. I had left my first husband after years of having an affair, having had a miscarriage and a baby from that affair. I had two children from my first marriage, and I had to look at the effects my choices had on them. I was in pain seeing how my children struggled with going back and forth between houses and trying to get used to a stepfather and the new life I had chosen for me.

I knew I could not change the past and I know God saw the turmoil and the repentance in my heart. He knew that all I wanted was to live a life pleasing to him, but I had messed up. I was trying to find a way beyond the garbage to come to a place I could even feel God wanted me anymore. To come to a place, I could even believe he desired me to walk this life with him. He was so gentle and loving with me during that time. I didn't deserve it, but we never do deserve the extent of his love for us. He pours it out on us anyway because He is pure goodness. One night he gave me a dream. In my dream, Jesus was kneeling on the kitchen floor and he was washing my dress in a pail full of blood. As I was watching him in the dream I was thinking, how is that going to wash my dress? It instantly changed to me wearing the most beautiful white dress. My words cannot describe how radiant the dress was but the best way I can say it was a gloriously silky, flowy pure white dress. I remember twirling in it during the dream and feeling the material. I woke up and it brought me to tears at the realization Jesus took that old stained and dirty life of mine and he transformed it into something beautiful. That image he gave me of what Jesus did for us all, moved me deeply, and transformed my heart.

It was hard to watch the consequences of my past fall on my children. It hurt my heart so deeply to see them deal with the pain and I prayed fervently to the Lord for healing for them. I would pray and ask how he could bring this family of mine together and make us closer. I was in prayer one day and really had completely surrendered myself as I was praying on this matter and the idea of moving to a new house with land and animals came to me. I was so adamant that we would stay in the house we were in for financial reasons, but it was too small for all of us, so the idea surprised me. I focused in on where I felt I was being directed and my heart really opened and warmed to the idea of moving. I had to meditate on it with God for a little while before I approached my husband. I told him I had been praying for our family and I feel like God gave me a solution and shared about moving. He was closed because of finances so he told me maybe in a few years. I told him I believe God is calling us to it now. He was not open to the idea.

I continued to pray to the Lord on the matter and God continued my heart in that direction so I finally got an idea from the Lord and I said, "Honey, would you just open your heart up to the possibility? Would you please just consider the idea that if God is really calling us to move, that he would then provide all that is necessary for that move to happen?" And wouldn't you know….he said "Yes." I knew that all he had to do was be open and God would do the rest!

It took a few months before we were able to get the house on the market. It took a few months and it was sold. During that time, we were looking at houses with not too many prospects. A lot of homes were too much money and would not fit our family's needs. During the 60-day window for closing the pressure increased. Throughout the process I was very diligently praying that the Lord would lead us to the exact house he had in mind for us. We had specific needs for distance from the children's schools we were trying to accommodate. I was focused on listening intently for direction from the Lord. One night I had this dream of a yellow house. When I woke up, I was very excited! I felt like God had showed me direction and I quickly rolled over and told my husband about my dream. I thought it was one we already looked at. He said, "Sure! Let's ride our bicycles over there." He was trying to motivate me to ride with him and I gladly agreed. We rode the few miles over to the neighborhood and right up to the property and stopped to stare at the beautiful yellow house. I stood there quiet and a little perplexed. This house was not the house in my dream. Yes, they both were yellow, but this house was nothing like the one I had dreamed. I was very disappointed and confused. My husband suggested we keep riding through the neighborhood. I was agreeable and we chatted and rode as we discussed houses we liked and didn't like and why. We were having a lot of fun as we came to a street with two houses for sale signs right next to each other off in the distance. We headed down the street right to them.

I definitely remember the amazement I had when I first set my sights on the second house for sale. It was yellow and I couldn't believe how much it reminded me of my dream. I told my husband this one looks like the one in my dream! I was so excited that I checked the listing on my phone. I told my husband this must NOT be the one in my dream because it is not the price we can afford. I was sad but shrugged it off and moved on. We continued our search and ended up putting in offers on other homes. They were not being accepted and I was always not sure they were the right thing. We were continuing to get closer to our closing date and wondering what we would do with all our stuff and where to stay. It was becoming more stressful each day. I continued with my prayers asking God to be really clear with where he wanted us to be and I always went back to the knowledge he called me to this, so he does have this handled. With only three weeks left, we knew we would have to get a storage unit and probably just move in with my sister's family until we found something. We were getting a little disheartened.

About a week later I was driving in the car and my friend called to check up on me. She asked how the house hunt was going and I told her we didn't find anything that seemed to fit. She asked if I was asking God for specifics and to really get before him and ask Him for some clear details, if I had not been doing that already. Then she said, "Unless God shows you in a dream, you need to just keep praying for specifics!" We finished our conversation and I was meditating on her advice for me and the words just kept echoing in my head "Unless God shows you in a dream"…I kept hearing it over and over. I said out loud, "Well God, you showed me that yellow house in a dream, but that house was not in our price range." I was picturing the house and I couldn't get that house out of my mind. When I reached my destination, I was compelled to look up that house again. It had dropped in price by $30,000. Now that was still almost $30,000 over our max budget. I had the thought if they dropped it that much, maybe they would drop it even more! I called my sister, my real estate agent, and asked her to inquire on the property. She called the owners and they said they had gotten an offer for the house and had to have a decision in two days. We set up an appointment to see the house the next day. We went to view the property and the house felt like home. It was more than we were asking for by far, it was perfect for us. With another offer on the table and unsure as to how much the offer was, we went home to pray about what we could offer. I knew we could not offer the asking price, we could only offer what we had.

So, we did, but I felt compelled to include a letter. During the showing, it was the sister of the owner and she had told us how her dad had built this for her sister, and this was supposed to be their forever home. The owners had to move due to a job and that took them out of state. It made me fall in the love with the house even more knowing the house was already filled with such love and it was made with care. That piece meant a great deal to me. I expressed information on our family, how I felt about the house and that I really felt that God had shown me this house in a dream, and it felt like home. My sister called me back the following day and said that the owners countered our offer because they really wanted us to have the house. It was $20,000 more than we originally offered. I told my sister no, there was no way we could come up with that dollar amount. I cried after getting off the phone. I knew I had replied the right way, but I was feeling sad. Then I realized, if that house is meant to be ours, then I believe it will be! Things happen all the time with houses not closing as planned. Deals fall through so I just told God I believed him for his goodness and if he calls that house our home, then I believe him for it! I had a lot of peace and I released my sadness. I knew if that wasn't the house for us, then he would have something more fitting in store. My sister called the lady back and told her the news. Then my sister prayed for us, that the money would be there if the opportunity came and that he would make provision.

A few hours later my sister called me back. She said, "Colette, would there be any way you could come up with 5,000 more dollars so you could have that house?" I said, "YES! But what do you mean? What happened?" She told me she prayed for me about the provision and that then the owner called back and told her she had been praying for the person who would own this house. That it would be someone who would love it as much as she did. She really wanted our family to have the house, as the other family who had put in an offer had wanted to gut the house and redo most of it. She felt like I was the one she had been praying for to own this house. However, for this deal to work out, my sister would have to step out of the deal and not get her commission. Then they could lower the cost so that they would still get the same amount for their house and be at the price we could pay. My loving and incredibly generous sister said she would do that for me. I was overwhelmed by the love of my sister, the love and goodness of God.

Not only did we find the house just before we had to leave the other, it was vacant, and they were willing to let us rent the house until we could close on the sale. We could not have orchestrated anything to such perfection as God had done. We moved right from our old house to the new house within a weeks' time and that whole experience totally grew my faith with God! It was so clear how he called me and all I had to do was be obedient and believe him. He managed all the other pieces. It fascinates me to realize how complicated we can make things when God only desires, we trust him and let him simply do what he does…authors and perfects!

It made me realize how my approach to my heavenly father was so skewed. My approach had always been with my reasoning and thinking with my limited understanding of the complete picture and plan. Then I would desperately ask God to please bless the plan I made. God's way was so much better and when we follow in faith, the path he sets out for us always works out. After that experience with God, I wanted my whole life to look like that! I wanted to live differently. Never before had I known what a beautiful and amazing adventure life could be fearlessly following God! May I never stop moving with the Lord and may the Lord continue to increase my faith as he draws me to the destiny, he has called me to.

How did you stay motivated in a season where patience, faith, and trust had to be exercised?

Sometimes it can be very difficult to have forward movement with the Lord. I feel like I have gone through many seasons of being super close to God and then mediocrely walking through my life not intentionally making connection. I feel it is definitely a must to be intentional about my thinking, my choice for desiring God, and intentional with my time. When I get wrapped up in the busyness of life, I find it incredibly hard to be encouraged and walk closely with the Lord. I feel like all things that are not prioritized or intentioned get pushed back to the next day, and the next day. Pretty soon I have no idea how I could have gone a month without engaging with God. I experience great emotional upsets when I am not grounded in truth and I live out of emotion. It is very important for my journey with God to be spending time listening to him through the Bible and prayer, otherwise I get caught up in thinking like the world. I enjoy spending time completely quiet, just listening for God and praising him. I find respite and peace connecting with God.

Mentorship has been a pivotal piece for my faith. What a huge blessing for me to step under someone else who has walked through what I am going though and has made it to the other side, encouraging me. In my younger years, I did not understand the importance but as I began to grow with the Lord, I really saw the privilege of mentorship. I would pray about a mentor and then I would look at the fruit of the women, to see how their walk with God made them different.

They were able to come alongside me in spending time to get together to talk about life and the lessons they learned. God would reveal his truth during those conversations, and I would receive the wisdom they shared and apply it to my life.

I love listening to sermons on exactly where I am needing encouragement or wisdom. The internet is full of God's word for finding exactly what can speak to your heart on an issue you are going through. Please do not get me wrong, it does not always mean I always liked the truth I received but I know God's truth is always available to us if we seek him. We get to decide if we are putting those truths into practice. God is so faithful to bring forward the thing we most need to hear and sometimes we have no idea that is the very thing we are needing to help us walk out what God is calling us to just up ahead.

I love making a vision board – Habakkuk 2:2 states write the vision and make it plain so the heralds may run with it. I enjoy sitting and listening for God's direction in my year to come. To spend time with God and work with him to create his vision for the coming season or the coming year. I am a very visual person. So, it brings me a lot of peace and hope to have something that sits on my wall. I can look at it whenever I need to refocus or need a little encouragement that God has spoken to me. The knowledge that he desires to lead, and direct us is incredibly powerful. It helps me to continue to pray out those things on hard days and know that I need to bring all my thoughts captive to what Christ says, not on what the world says or what my current situation appears to be right now.

Praising God for all the promises he has already brought to pass is something I have to do when I grow weary or feel down about a situation. Gratitude changes my thinking and my heart almost instantly. It reminds and renews my spirit to a place of joy and peace. I also practice speaking out my belief in his truths and finding scripture to match the truths that attack the areas I am having trouble with at the moment. I go so far as to put them on sticky notes, white boards and even on my bathroom mirror with dry erase markers to have visual reminders so those scriptures ever present in my mind. I am so grateful God has taught me that my thinking transitions into what my life becomes. *"As a man thinketh in his heart, so he is."* Proverbs 23:7

I speak to the Lord with gratitude for all areas in my life. I look at the hard things I have had to walk through, and I ask him to show me the benefit and blessing that came out of those instances, even though at the time they did not feel good. He allows my heart to experience joy and gratitude when I take the time to be open to all his goodness. He has shown me how it produced the character necessary for my future, empathy for others in similar situations, and perseverance. For we know God works together for the good of those who love him, who have been called according to his purpose.

Praying with others is a huge blessing. God seems to do something remarkable in the hearts of those who pray together and come into agreement with each other's prayers. It is so powerful, and it does something to the heart when praying with someone else. I believe God so loves relationships and so when we are fellowshipping with each other and Him; which honors God.

What scriptures, books or resources do you recommend using when you are looking to grow in your walk with God?

I have continued to go back to a book called Dream Wild by Jennifer LeClaire. It has really spoken directly to my heart on truths about breaking down lies that have tried to keep me from following Gods direction for my life.

The Word of God is needed daily for me to be growing. Other people can write about what is in the bible but having the foundation of reading and ingesting God's word into my daily life is critical for my growth with him. I have found I read Hebrews and James very often. Isaiah 61 and Psalm 91 have made a huge impact for me.

I really enjoy women's bible study and the one that had a big impact is John Blackaby's Hearing the Voice of God. God used that study to help me connect very genuinely and openly with other woman and not mask who I was with who I thought people wanted me to be. It revealed how much God wants to interact with us if we would take the time to observe and see where he is working and moving, then choose to partner with him in what he is already doing.

Colette Huxtable

Colette Huxtable was born and raised in North Dakota, until she moved to Arizona for college and has now lived in Arizona for 18 years. Colette owns her own business Chemistry Coffee Roasting, she worked as a Registered Nurse in Oncology, and has interests in hiking, cooking, triathlon, and travel. She has a determined nature evident in her completion of the Ironman triathlon, and an acute attention to detail perfect for specialty coffee roasting. Colette lives on a small farm with her husband and four children.

Colette is passionate about genuine relationship and loving people is at the heart of everything she does on this life adventure of following God. She has maintained meaningful relationships with both co-workers and patients as a nurse, with the emotional demands of oncology she was well suited to be helpful both physically and emotionally. Colette's kind demeanor and peacefulness has helped her business grow and move forward, all while balancing her deep love for her family.

ChemistryCoffeeAZ@gmail.com

www.ChemistryCoffeeRoasting.com

What is your Yes, God moment?

Made in the USA
Columbia, SC
05 April 2019